Keynes' Monetary Thought

A study of its development

Keynes' Monetary Thought

A study of its development

Don Patinkin

The Hebrew University of Jerusalem

Duke University Press   Durham, North Carolina   1976

L.C.C. card no. 75-40630

I.S.B.N. 0-8223-0360-4

Printed in the United States
of America

אמר ר' חנינא
הרבה למדתי מרבותי
ומחברי יותר מרבותי
ומתלמידי יותר מכולם
תענית ז, א

לזכר תלמידי
אבנר בן־אליעזר ויואב ברום
שנפלו במלחמת יום־הכיפורים

Rabbi Chanina said:
I have learned much from my teachers
from my colleagues more than from my teachers
and most of all from my students.
    Babylonian Talmud, Taanit 7:a

To the memory of my students
Avner Ben-Eliezer and Yoav Brum
who fell in the Yom Kippur War
October 1973

Contents

Acknowledgments

As indicated in the Introduction, the immediate occasion for writing this essay is the appearance of Keynes' major writings on monetary theory in the edition of *The Collected Writings of John Maynard Keynes* which is now being published by the Royal Economic Society under the general editorship of Sir Austin Robinson. Let me accordingly first express my sincerest appreciation to the Society for generously granting me permission to cite at length from the various volumes of this edition.

Despite the wealth of material presented in this edition, I have felt the need at various points in this essay to obtain supplementary information, as well as additional unpublished documents from the Keynes Papers, which are deposited in the Marshall Library of Cambridge University. In this connection, I cannot adequately express my gratitude to Lord Kahn (who is Keynes' executor) and also to Donald Moggridge (who edited Volumes XIII and XIV of the *Collected Writings* from the aforementioned Papers) for the unfailing spirit of scholarly cooperation with which they patiently and expeditiously met my every request for assistance. I am also indebted to Lord Kahn for permission to cite the unpublished documents that were so supplied.

Most of the material in this essay was first presented and further developed in the seminar on the history of modern monetary thought which I have given at the Hebrew University during the past three years. As always, it is a pleasure to express my deep gratitude and indebtedness to the students of these seminars for their many valuable criticisms and suggestions. But it is a pleasure mixed with sadness: for among the most active participants in these seminar-discussions were Avner Ben-Eliezer and Yoav Brum.

An earlier version of this essay was circulated in the fall of 1974, and I have benefited greatly from the stimulating comments and criticisms which I then received from many individuals. In this context my debt is particularly great to Sir John Hicks, with whom I spent many pleasant and extremely fruitful hours discussing the manuscript at a conference convened by the Latsis Foundation in September 1974 at Nafplion, Greece—for quite other purposes! These invaluable discussions were followed by a further highly illuminating correspondence with Sir John on various points.

1

This early version was also much improved as a result of stimulating and valuable discussions of it (carried out mostly by means of correspondence) with William Baumol, Stanley Fischer, Donald Moggridge, and Donald Winch. Again, I derived much help and stimulation from the critical comments on this version that were made by three referees. On various points, I was also greatly aided by the comments and advice of my colleagues Chaim Barkai, Yoram Ben-Porath, and Ephraim Kleiman.

The material of this essay also served as the subject of the graduate seminar which I have given at the University of Western Ontario during my successive month-long visits there in the past two years. I would like to thank Kevin Burley, Joel Fried, and Peter Howitt for the helpful comments I received from them in the course of these visits.

I would also like to express my warm appreciation to Elizabeth Johnson (who has edited several volumes of Keynes' *Collected Writings*) for the many illuminating conversations that I had with her. And I have a special debt to Harry Johnson for encouraging me to publish this essay as a separate monograph. Needless to say, none of the individuals who have been mentioned here is to be held responsible for the views expressed in this essay.

Any study of this kind necessarily entails a heavy burden of library work and checking of texts and references. Here I have been blessed with a succession of excellent research assistants whose help has been invaluable: Leonardo Leiderman and Gabriella Brenner, as well as (in the preliminary stages of the work) Akiva Offenbacher. To all of them I am deeply indebted for the gratifying responsibility and accuracy with which they carried out their tasks, as well as for the many valuable comments and suggestions which they have provided.

Similarly, I owe a special debt to Mrs. Vera Jacobs, who has loyally and conscientiously devoted herself—with great care, accuracy, and patience—to typing this essay through its many drafts and revisions. Her pleasant and most efficient help has greatly lightened the burden of preparing this essay. I am also indebted to Mrs. Margaret Gower and her staff at the University of Western Ontario for the typing assistance which they have so expeditiously provided during my successive visits to that university.

Thanks are also due to the registrars and other officials of various colleges at Cambridge and Oxford, who have kindly provided some of the information used in the description of the dramatis personae which appears below.

I would like now to express my sincerest appreciation to the Ford Foundation for a grant received through the Israel Foundation Trustees which enabled me to devote my free time to work on this essay. Grants to cover the costs of research and typing assistance were received in the first stage of this work from the Central Research Fund of the Hebrew University, and in subsequent stages from the Israel Commission for Basic Research—and I am most indebted to them. I am also grateful to the Maurice Falk Institute for Economic Research in Israel and to the Van Leer Jerusalem Foundation for the kind assistance they have provided throughout this work.

Let me also express my thanks to the editors of the *Economic Journal* for their kind permission to reproduce in Chapter 2 of this essay much of my review article on "The Collected Writings of John Maynard Keynes: From the *Tract* to the *General Theory*," which appeared in the June 1975 issue of the *Journal*.

I would like finally to express my deepest appreciation to the Israel Academy of Sciences and Humanities, whose quiet studies, overlooking the southern hills of Jerusalem, have provided the ideal scholarly atmosphere for carrying out the work on this essay.

Jerusalem, July 1975   Don Patinkin

Dramatis personae as of 1931[1]

John Maynard Keynes. Age 48. Educated at Eton and King's College, Cambridge. Specialized in mathematics and took his B.A. in 1905. Afterwards, spent an additional year at Cambridge studying economics under Alfred Marshall (1842–1924) and A.C. Pigou. Fellow of King's College from 1909 onwards. [(a),(e)]

Arthur C. Pigou. Age 54. Educated at Harrow and King's College, Cambridge. Studied first history and then economics. Took his B.A. in 1899. Fellow of King's College from 1902 and onwards. Succeeded Marshall as Professor of Political Economy in 1908, at the young age of 31. Was one of Keynes' teachers. [(a),(e),(k)]

Ralph G. Hawtrey. Age 52. Educated at Eton and Trinity College, Cambridge. Specialized in mathematics and took his B.A. in 1901. Afterwards entered the civil service and worked at the Treasury in London from 1904 onwards. Acquired his knowledge of economics not at Cambridge (he never attended even one of Marshall's lectures), but at the Treasury. An acquaintance of Keynes's since the latter's student days at Cambridge. [(a),(e),(i)]

Dennis H. Robertson. Age 41. Educated at Eton and Trinity College, Cambridge. Specialized first in classics, taking his B.A. in 1910. Then went on to study economics under Pigou and Keynes, the latter serving as his director of studies. Fellow of Trinity College from 1914 onwards. Collaborated closely with Keynes during 1920's, and especially in the writing of his (Robertson's) *Banking Policy and the Price Level* (1926). [(a),(f),(i)]

Richard F. Kahn. Age 26. Educated St. Paul's School and King's College, Cambridge. Specialized first in mathematics and physics, taking his B.A. in 1927. Then studied economics as a pupil of Keynes. Fellow of King's College from 1930 onwards. [(b),(k)]

Joan Robinson. Age 28. Educated St. Paul's Girls' School, London, and Girton College, Cambridge. Specialized in economics and took her B.A. in 1925. Appointed Assistant Lecturer in Economics at Cambridge in 1931. [(b),(e),(i)]

Austin Robinson. Age 34. Educated Marlborough College and Christ College, Cambridge. Took his B.A. in 1920. Fellow of Corpus Christi College, Cambridge, 1924–26. Appointed University Lec-

1. In approximate order of appearance.

turer at Cambridge in 1929. Fellow of Sidney Sussex College, Cambridge, from 1931 onwards. [(b),(e),(i)]

Roy F. Harrod. Age 31. Educated Westminster School and New College, Oxford. Specialized in classics, philosophy, and history, completing undergraduate studies in 1922. Lecturer at Christ Church, Oxford 1922–24. Student of Christ Church from 1924 onwards. Visited Cambridge during 1922–23 in order to study economics under Keynes. [(b),(e),(i)]

James E. Meade. Age 24. Educated Malvern College and Oriel College, Oxford. Studied classics and P.P.E., taking his B.A. in 1930. Fellow and Lecturer in Economics, Hertford College, Oxford, from 1930. Visited Trinity College, Cambridge, in 1930–31. [(b),(e),(i)]

Piero Sraffa. Age 33. Educated University of Turin. First known to Keynes as translator of his *Tract on Monetary Reform* into Italian (1924). In 1927 was brought to Cambridge from Italy by Keynes, who was also instrumental in having him made a member of the King's high table. Appointed University Lecturer in Economics in 1927, but resigned lectureship in 1931, though continued as Librarian, Marshall Library, Cambridge. [(b),(e),(i),(k),(l)]

Friedrich A. von Hayek. Age 32. Educated Vienna University. Director Austrian Institute for Economic Research 1927–31. Lecturer in Economics, Vienna University, 1929–31. Moved in 1931 to England where, as Professor at the London School of Economics, played a crucial role in spreading the influence of Austrian and Wicksellian economics in England. [(b),(h)]

Gunnar Myrdal. Age 33. Educated Stockholm University. Lecturer in Political Economy at Stockholm University from 1927. [(c)]

John R. Hicks. Age 27. Educated Clifton College and Balliol College, Oxford. Studied P.P.E. and took his B.A. in 1925. Lecturer, London School of Economics from 1926. Did not have any significant contacts with Keynes until after publication of the *General Theory*. [(b),(g),(j)]

Bertil Ohlin. Age 32. Educated Harvard University (A.M. 1923) and Stockholm University (Ph.D. 1924). Professor University of Copenhagen, 1925–29. Debated German reparations transfer problem with Keynes in pages of 1929 *Economic Journal*. [(d)]

Sources: (a) *International Encyclopedia of the Social Sciences* (1973). (b) *Who's Who 1973* (A & C Black Ltd., London). (c) *The International Who's Who 1967–68* (Europa Publications Ltd., London). (d) *Directory of Members of the American Economic Association, A.E.R.* 64 (Oct. 1974). (e) Harrod (1951). (f) Hicks

(1966). (g) Hicks (1973). (h) Robbins (1971). (i) College registrar records. (j) Personal correspondence with Sir John Hicks. (k) Personal correspondence with Lord Kahn. (l) *Tract*, p. xii, n.1.

1. Introduction

The *Tract*, the *Treatise*, and the *General Theory*: this is the inter-war trilogy that marks the development of John Maynard Keynes' monetary thought from the quantity-theory tradition that he had in-herited from his teachers at Cambridge; to his subsequent systematic attempt to dynamize and elaborate upon this theory and its applica-tions; and, finally, to the revolutionary work which he wrote under the constant stimulus and criticism of his colleagues and students —and with which he changed the face of monetary theory and defined its developmental framework for years to come.

The story of this development has been told many times.[1] The occasion for turning to it again in this essay is the reissue of these classic volumes, together with two companion volumes of related and hitherto largely unpublished materials, as part of the magnificent edi-tion of Keynes' *Collected Writings* that the Royal Economic Society is publishing as its most appropriate memorial to him. In particular, in Volumes XIII and XIV of these *Writings*, entitled *The General Theory and After*, Donald Moggridge has ably collected, edited, and reproduced from the voluminous Keynes' Papers a great variety of materials (including lectures and reports, extensive correspondence, fragments of earlier drafts, scribbled notes, and corrected galley proofs, not to speak of Keynes' many published articles) that are connected with Keynes' work on these volumes. This, then, is an appropriate occasion to reread the trilogy all together, against the edifying background of these new materials, and thus to obtain an overview of the development of Keynes' thinking on monetary prob-lems during the fifteen-year period that culminated in the appearance of the *General Theory*.[2]

---

1. Most notably, by E.A.G. Robinson (1947), Klein (1947), Harrod (1951), and Shackle (1967).

2. The full titles of the volumes referred to here are these: *A Tract on Monetary Reform* (1923, 1971), *A Treatise on Money, Vol. I. The Pure Theory of Money* (1930, 1971), *A Treatise on Money: Vol II. The Applied Theory of Money* (1930, 1971), *The General Theory of Employment, Interest, and Money* (1936, 1973), *The General Theory and After: Part I. Preparation*, ed. Donald Moggridge (1973), and *The General Theory and After: Part II. Defence and Development*, ed. Donald Moggridge (1973). For con-venience, I shall refer to these volumes by the following short titles, respectively: *Tract*: *Treatise* I or *TM* I; *Treatise* II or *TM* II; *General Theory* or *GT*; *JMK* XIII; and *JMK* XIV. I shall also use *JMK* I, *JMK* II, and so forth to refer to the other volumes in

In presenting this overview, I shall, of course, describe the distinguishing analytical characteristics of each of Keynes' three major works. My concern, however, is not only with the *Tract*, *Treatise*, and *General Theory* as separate entities, but even more with the ideational relationships between them. Thus I will be interested in describing the different intellectual objectives that Keynes set for himself in these successive books—and the way in which the objectives of one book were affected by the reception accorded to the preceding one. I will be interested in the ideas, explicit and implicit, that are common to all three books; in the ideas that were modified in the course of writing them, the nature of the modifications, and Keynes' reasons for making them; and in the ideas that continued to influence Keynes' thinking even though he believed he had sloughed them off. And over and above all this I will be interested in the role of discussion and criticism in generating these developments.

Needless to say, my account of these developments will be based on an examination of the relevant texts. In this way I hope to present Keynes' works as he himself saw them. With this purpose in mind, I shall frequently support my account with extensive quotations, making every effort to interpret them within their proper contexts.

Similarly, in my discussion of the relevant texts, I shall adhere to their language and terminology and will try to avoid the temptation to translate them into modern concepts. For we run the risk of distorting the original intention of Keynes' writings if we try to view them through analytical lenses that are more sophisticated and more finely ground that those that he was wont to use. In any event, my purpose is not to engage in speculation about what Keynes might have said or should have said about current issues in monetary theory; it is instead to the best of my ability to present to the reader a documented interpretation of what he did say.

Let me now emphasize that this essay is not intended as a comprehensive study of all aspects of Keynes' monetary thought during this period. Thus my primary focus—like that of *JMK* XIII and XIV—is on the development of the *General Theory*. Now, for reasons to be explained in the next chapter, the *General Theory* is a book that deals with a closed economy. Correspondingly, I shall in this essay barely touch upon those parts of the *Tract* and *Treatise* that deal with international monetary economics—even though this was one of Keynes' major concerns throughout his life, and in these two books in particular.

---

this edition of *Collected Writings*. Needless to say, all page references in this essay will be to the new edition of these books.

Again, I deal only with certain aspects of the development of Keynes' thinking about monetary policy. First, any thorough study of this development should be integrated into a systematic account of the contemporaneous historical developments, and the presentation of such an account would carry me too far afield. Second, even though, as will be emphasized in the next chapter, Keynes' concern with current policy questions was the major impetus for his professional writings, his main vehicle for discussing these questions publicly were his frequent contributions to the influential highbrow periodicals of the day. Again, one of the most effective ways in which Keynes gave expression to his policy views was through the leading, if not dominating, roles that he played in such official bodies as the famous Macmillan Committee and the Economic Advisory Council.[3] Accordingly a full reexamination of the development of Keynes' policy thinking over the years had best await the publication of the materials relating to these activities in the forthcoming volumes of his *Collected Writings*.

Another limitation of this essay is that it generally treats the discussions and criticisms reflected in the relevant texts as if they were interactions between disembodied intellects. There is no attempt —and it would indeed be beyond my competence to make such an attempt—to discuss the psychological and sociological influences that were undoubtedly at work here. But in order to remind ourselves that we are nevertheless dealing with interactions that took place between human beings—interactions which were undoubtedly influenced by such factors as relative age, communality or difference of backgrounds, student-teacher relationships, and the like—I have prefaced this essay with a list of the principal dramatis personae, providing some minimal information on these points. This list also briefly indicates the nature of the specific connections that were respectively woven between some of these individuals and Keynes even before our story begins.

Let me also note that, even if it were possible to do so, I have not attempted to survey the vast literature that has grown up over the years on the interpretation of Keynes' monetary writings. On the other hand, in the natural course of this essay, I have also dealt with the major issues raised by this literature: the conceptual framework of the *Treatise* and of the "fundamental equations" in particular; the by now legendary process of fruitful discussion and criticism which first expressed itself in the "arguing out" of the *Treatise* after its publica-

3. See Harrod (1951) and Winch (1969). See also the forthcoming study by Howson and Winch (1976).

tion, and which subsequently accompanied every stage of the development of the *General Theory*; the respective roles in this process of Keynes and his critics; the relationship between the *Treatise* and the *General Theory*; the chronology of the development of the theory of effective demand; the conceptual framework of the *General Theory* and the nature of its basic assumptions; Keynes' analytical style; the validity of the income-expenditure IS-LM representation of the *General Theory*; and the like.

In most cases, I do not think that my views on these issues differ basically from the traditional ones, and this is particularly true for those issues on which the traditional interpretation has in recent years been challenged by newer ones. In any event, out of a desire to avoid polemics, I have not generally indicated the points of agreement and disagreement with other writers. All I have attempted to do is to provide the reader with the textual evidence on which I have based my own conclusions on the questions at issue.

Finally, I am sure there is no need for me to emphasize that I have in this essay discussed—and even then not completely—only some of the problems that arise in one's mind as one rereads Keynes' monetary trilogy together with its two companion volumes. This is particularly true with respect to the latter: for *JMK* XIII and XIV are verily a widow's cruse from which students of the development of Keynes' thought will continue to draw materials for years to come—without any diminution in the profits to scholarship.

2. Differences and similarities: some general observations[1]

Though I have referred to Keynes' three books on monetary theory as a trilogy, they differ from each other greatly not only in substance (a difference that has, of course, been a major theme of all studies of the development of Keynes' thought) but also in form and purpose. Thus the *Tract* is not really a book, but a short and somewhat unsystematic revision and elaboration of the series of articles on postwar economic policy that Keynes first published in 1922 in the "Reconstruction Supplements" of the *Manchester Guardian Commercial*. And one of the advantages of the present edition of the *Tract* is that it makes this relationship unmistakably clear by means of the variorum readings from these articles that it appends to the text.

In the *Tract*—as in these articles—Keynes dealt with the pressing problems of inflation, deflation, and exchange rate disequilibrium that then beset Europe. On the other hand, the brief, formal presentation of monetary theory that appears in the *Tract* (see Chapter 3 below)—and which, as Keynes tells us (*Tract*, p. 63, n.1) "follows the general lines of Professor Pigou . . . and of Dr. Marshall"—is part of the material that Keynes added to these articles in making up the book. And just as this theoretical material was (by Keynes' "revealed preference") not necessary for an understanding of the original articles, so is it not really necessary for the book; its deletion would interfere very little with an understanding of the argument of the *Tract* at other points.[2] Conversely—and this is one of the clearest manifestations of the failure of the *Tract* to be an integrated whole —this added theoretical material on pages 61–70 barely reflects the penetrating and elegant analysis of inflation as a tax on real money balances[3] that Keynes reproduces from the aforementioned articles on pages 37–53 of the *Tract*.

1. This chapter reproduces, with some minor deletions and changes, Sections II–V and VII of my review article on "The Collected Writings of John Maynard Keynes: From the *Tract* to the *General Theory*" (1975).
2. Correspondingly, the theoretical pages of the *Tract* received little if any attention in most of the reviews of the book at the time. Thus see Angell (1925), Hawtrey (1924), Owens (1924), and Sprague (1924); only Gregory's review (1924) was something of an exception.
3. Including the notion of an optimum rate of inflation from the viewpoint of maximizing tax receipts! (*Tract* pp. 43–45).

Nor does the *Tract* incorporate the dynamic analysis of the way in which an influx of gold operates through the banking system—and thence on prices—that Keynes (basing himself on Marshall) had summarized in his 1911 review of Irving Fisher's *Purchasing Power of Money*.[4] Thus the *Tract*—as a theoretical work—is not only not integrated within itself, but it even fails to reflect some major aspects of Keynes' thinking about monetary problems at the time it was published.

On both of these scores the *Treatise* is the exact opposite. It is as specifically designed for a professional audience with a major concern with the latest development in monetary theory as the *Tract* was designed for a general audience primarily concerned with current policy. Indeed, from the viewpoint of traditional scholarship, the *Treatise* is Keynes' most ambitious and weighty work: the two-volume work—on "The Pure Theory of Money" and "The Applied Theory of Money"—designed to establish firmly his academic reputation. At its core (in Books III–IV of Volume I) is a formal, rigorous presentation of a theory of money that deals in detail with both the static and dynamic aspects of the problem. And in the slow, methodical, dignified, and comprehensive manner in which an academic treatise customarily proceeds—but in which Keynes of the interwar period so rarely proceeded[5]—it leads up to this core, first, by defining the nature of money and describing its historical origins (Book I); and then (in Book II) describing at length the various index numbers that can be used to measure the value of money, which (to use one of Keynes' favorite terms) is the *quaesitum* of monetary theory. And afterwards comes Volume II, which begins with a lengthy description of the respective empirical magnitudes of the critical theoretical variables described in the preceding volume—as well as of the institutional features of the financial sectors which bear upon these variables (Books V–VI). Only when all this is completed does Keynes finally proceed (in Book VII) to a systematic presentation of the monetary policy, both domestic and international, that he derives from his theory (see Chapters 4–6 below).

The *General Theory*, too, is—in Keynes' words of his preface—"chiefly addressed to . . . fellow economists" (*GT* p. xxi). It differs from the *Treatise* in being almost exclusively concerned with theory. Indeed, this is the whole purpose of the book, as indicated by its very title. Thus the *General Theory* contains practically no de-

4. I would consider this long review essentially to be Keynes' first published writing on monetary theory.

5. See below, n. 22.

scription of institutional details. And for a work that is credited with having initiated a revolution in fiscal policy, it contains surprisingly few explicit discussions of the policy implications of its analysis. Indeed, the major new policy conclusion of the *General Theory* as compared with the *Treatise*—namely, that monetary policy directed at varying the interest rate might not be enough, and that an effective full-employment policy may well require direct government spending—is never developed systematically and in detail. Instead, it is only referred to on one or two occasions in passing (e.g., *GT* p. 164) and in brief "Concluding Notes" of a general nature (*GT* pp. 372–84). Similarly, the problem of the international monetary system—which was one of Keynes' major concerns in both the *Tract* and the *Treatise* (as it was once again to be at Bretton Woods after World War II)—is barely mentioned in the *General Theory*.[6] I shall return to this point below in this chapter.

I should, however, emphasize that if from these viewpoints the *General Theory of Employment, Interest, and Money* was more narrowly conceived than the *Treatise on Money*, from another viewpoint it is—as its title indicates—much broader. For as I have already hinted, "monetary theory" in the *Treatise* means, first and foremost, a theory that explains the determination of the price level. Accordingly, if the argument of the *Treatise* revolves about Keynes' "fundamental equations," these are (as the title of its Chapter 10 makes clear) "The Fundamental Equations *for the Value of Money*" (*TM* I, p. 120; italics added). Again, Keynes explains the absence of a full analysis of the role of wage changes in these equations on the grounds that "this is a treatise on money, and not on the wages system" (*TM* I, p. 151). Similarly, he prefaces Book VI of the *Treatise*, "The Rate of Investment and Its Fluctuations," with the statement that it is "in the nature of a digression, which is doubtfully in place in a treatise on money" (*TM* II, p. 85). In conformity with this view—and in sharp contrast with the systematic attempt of the *General Theory* to base its analysis on the concepts of value theory—the term "marginal productivity" (of labor or of capital) does not appear in the *Treatise*. Correspondingly (as we shall see in Chapter 7 below) one of the first signposts on the road that leads from the *Treatise* to the *General Theory* is Keynes' change of the title of his autumn 1932 lectures from "The Pure Theory of Money" (which was the title he had used since

6. Aside from the references to the balance of payments in the "Notes on Mercantilism" in Chapter 23 of the *General Theory*—a chapter which is, after all, only an appendage to the main body of the book—the only references to an open economy that I have been able to find are the passing ones on pp. 121–22 and 270.

1929–30) to "The Monetary Theory of Production" (*JMK* XIII, pp. 343, 411–12).

Not that the *Treatise* was not concerned with changes in production. On the contrary, its main purpose was to explain the cyclical fluctuations of production and hence employment that then beset the economies of Europe and the United States. But the theory developed in the *Treatise* analyzed these fluctuations not directly, but as the consequence of prior changes in prices, which were the subject of the fundamental equations. Furthermore, what distinguishes the *General Theory* from the *Treatise* is not simply its more direct and precise concern with changes in output, but the crucial role that it assigns to such changes as an *equilibrating force* with respect to aggregate demand and supply—or, equivalently, with respect to saving and investment. Indeed, this is what Keynes' theory of effective demands is all about. I shall elaborate upon these points in Chapters 4 and 8 below.

Despite the foregoing differences between Keynes' three books on monetary economics, there are also important similarities. Thus a common element of these books is their concern with practical policy problems—and their related concern with the empirical aspects of these problems. At the same time I must emphasize that Keynes (like most of his contemporaries) largely used empirical data for illustrative purposes—or at most as a basis for rather impressionistic observations about the relations between the variables described by the data. Though there are partial exceptions (see the second paragraph below), Keynes practically never carried out a systematic statistical analysis of empirical data as a basis for conclusions.

Thus, for example, Keynes' excellent presentation of the purchasing-power-parity theory in the *Tract* is supported by charts and diagrams showing the generally corresponding movements of the actual exchange rates of England, France, and Italy with those respectively predicted by the theory (*Tract*, pp. 81–86). Similarly, Keynes' aforementioned analysis of inflation as a tax on real cash balances—and his explanation that this tax will decrease the volume of these balances that individuals will be willing to hold—is illustrated by data from the postwar hyperinflations of Germany, Austria, and Russia (*Tract*, pp. 45–46). Similarly, in the second, "applied" volume of his *Treatise*, Keynes presents empirical estimates of the variables that play a key role in the theory he developed in the first volume: namely, the quantity of money, the velocity of circulation, the volume of working capital—and he even adds a long chapter (30) providing historical illustrations of his theory.

Though there is less emphasis on empirical data in the *General*

Theory, it is noteworthy that Keynes was quick to make use in it of Simon Kuznets' preliminary estimates of net investment in the United States in order to illustrate his (Keynes') basic contention about the critical role of wide fluctuations in this variable in generating business cycles (*GT* pp. 102–5). What is even more noteworthy is Keynes' use of these data in order to make an empirical estimate (crude as it was) of the magnitude of the multiplier in the United States—and thence of the marginal propensity to consume of that country (*GT* pp. 127–28). Thus Keynes not only made the marginal propensity to consume a central component of macroeconomic theory but (to the best of my knowledge)[7] also provided the first estimate of its magnitude that was based on an examination of statistical time series![8]

Though all three of Keynes' books are concerned with policy issues, they nevertheless differ in the extent and sense of immediacy with which their policy discussions are presented. In view of the origin of the *Tract* in articles in the *Manchester Guardian*, it is not surprising that discussions on current policy issues are paramount in it. Indeed, having only a short time before dealt so successfully with prime ministers in his *Economic Consequences of the Peace* (1919, *JMK* II) and in his *Revision of the Treaty* (1922, *JMK* III), Keynes had no hesitations in sending out directly from the pages of the *Tract* advice on current matters to the finance ministers (or their equivalent), not only of England and the United States but also of Czechoslovakia (p. 120), Germany (pp. 50–52), and France (pp. xxi–xxii).[9]

In contrast—as befits a comprehensive, scientific work—Keynes' policy recommendations of the *Treatise* are for the most part of a more general nature, though here too there are references to specific, immediate issues (e.g., *TM* II, pp. 270 ff, 348 ff). Least specific in its

---

7. Unfortunately, the statistical basis of Richard Kahn's original estimate of this propensity in his celebrated article on the multiplier (1931, pp. 13–14) is not specified —except to say that it was supplied by Colin Clark.

8. Thus Keynes' later (1944–45) serving as president of the Econometric Society was not simply honorific. Students of the history of econometric methods will also find it interesting to note that by deriving his estimate of the marginal propensity to consume from that of the multiplier, Keynes essentially estimated the former by means of the reduced-form method—and thus was (though obviously unknowingly) also the first to use this method of estimation! The significance of the "statistical revolution" that accompanied and interacted with the "Keynesian revolution" to their great mutual benefit is well attested by the fact that estimates of the overall volume of investment were not available only a few years before at the time when Keynes wrote his *Treatise* and had to make do instead with "partial indicators" (*TM* II, p. 87). For further discussion of this question, see my forthcoming paper on "Keynes and Econometrics: On the Interaction Between Macroeconomic Theory and Measurement in the Interwar Period" (1976).

9. These pages are from the preface to the French edition of the *Tract*, which appeared in 1924.

policy proposals is the *General Theory*—though it clearly reflects the threatening air of immediate crisis generated by the mass unemployment of the period.

What were the specific policy problems that concerned Keynes? Naturally enough, they varied with the contemporary situation. Indeed, as a first approximation they can be read off the curves in Fig. 2.1 describing the major economic developments in England during the period spanned by Keynes' three books.[10] Thus I have already mentioned Keynes' brilliant analysis in the *Tract* of postwar hyperinflation. But even countries (like England) that had not suffered disastrous extremes of hyperinflation in the postwar period, had nevertheless experienced years of rapid inflation that were followed by equally sharp deflations (*Tract*, p. 3). And against this background there emerged the problem of reestablishing an appropriate system of exchange rates among these countries.

This was one of the major problems that Keynes discussed in the *Tract*. In the course of this discussion he provided a lucid analysis (*Tract*, pp. 125–40) of the basic dilemma between the "alternative aims" of stability of the internal price level and stability of the exchange rate—and strongly argued the view that he was to reaffirm in the *Treatise* in favor of giving precedence to the aim of internal price stability. It was this view that also guided Keynes in the battle he waged in the mid-1920's against England's return to the gold standard at the prewar exchange rate.[11]

The problem of the relation between internal price levels and exchange rates—and indeed the whole problem of the international monetary system, and of the impact of domestic policies on international reserves in particular—are not discussed in the *General Theory*. The explanation for this fact too probably lies in the situation that prevailed in the Western world during the period that the *General Theory* was being written. In particular, this was the new world ushered in by England's abandonment of the gold standard in September 1931: a world of flexible exchange rates and/or severe restrictions on the flow of international trade, in which the aforementioned problems had accordingly largely lost their relevance.[12]

10. I should note that the data on which these curves are based were available to Keynes at the time he wrote and that he indeed referred to most of them (cf., e.g., *TM* I, p. 55; II, pp. 159, 318).

11. See especially his *Economic Consequences of Mr. Churchill* (1925). For a detailed study of this famous historical episode, including Keynes' role in it, see Moggridge, *British Monetary Policy 1924–1931* (1972). See also Winch (1969), chap. 5.

12. On the details of this world, see the classic study by Nurkse (1944). In this context it is also worth noting that Winch's study (1969) of economics and policy in

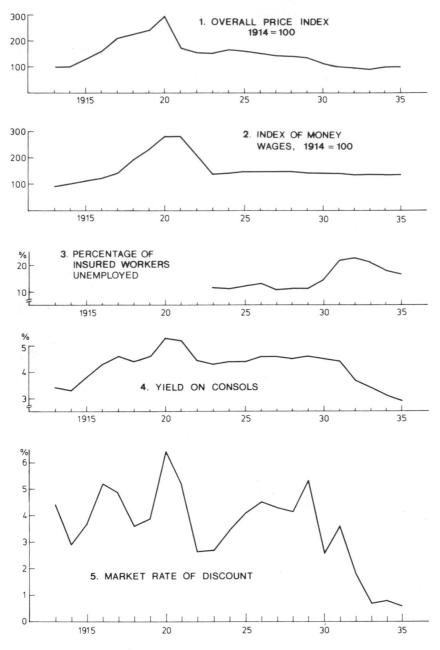

Fig. 2.1. Major economic developments in the United Kingdom, 1913–1935.
Source: Mitchell and Deane (1962). For chart 1, pp. 474–75; for chart 2,
pp. 344–45; for chart 3, p. 67; for chart 4, p. 455; and for chart 5, p. 460.

18

On the other hand, a problem that runs like a common thread throughout Keynes' trilogy is that of unemployment. As I shall show in Chapter 12 below, Keynes' changing views on the appropriate policies for dealing with this problem reflected both the changing situation (viz., the duration and depth of the unemployment, as well as the just described change in the framework of international economic relations) and his not entirely unrelated changing views on the validity of the quantity theory. Indeed, there are many who see Keynes' trilogy as The Saga of Man's Struggle for Freedom from the Quantity Theory—and I think there can be little doubt that Keynes himself so saw it.[13] Thus, as already noted, in the *Tract* Keynes embraced the Cambridge cash-balance form of this theory that he had received from his teachers. In the *Treatise* (as I shall explain in Chapter 5 below) he continued to maintain the quantity theory in a macroeconomic (though not microeconomic) context, but criticized it as being restricted in its validity to comparative-statics analysis; accordingly, Keynes considered its supplementation by an appropriate dynamic analysis to be one of his major objectives in the book. Finally, in the *General Theory* Keynes abandoned the quantity theory entirely, and in its place put the new theory that he had just developed. I shall return to this point in Chapter 11.

There is one point that I would like to make about the relationship between theory and policy in the *Treatise* and in the *General Theory*. It seems to me that in both cases the major contribution of the book is with respect to theory—and the purpose of the theory is to provide a rigorous underpinning for a policy position which already had many adherents. As Keynes himself indicated in Chapter 13 of the *Treatise*, this was certainly true for the bank-rate policy he advocated in that work. And as emphasized in recent years,[14] it is also true of the public-works-expenditure policy advocated by Keynes in the *General Theory*. Indeed, Keynes himself had already advocated such a policy in his famous 1929 election pamphlet (written with Hubert Henderson) *Can Lloyd George Do It?* (*JMK* IX, pp. 86–125). Accordingly,

England records many discussions of balance-of-payment problems during the decade that preceded the 1931 devaluation, but none in the years that immediately followed. See also Winch's reference to Harry D. White's report after a visit to Britain in 1935 that there was then "a complete lack of interest in British business circles in exchange problems" (Winch 1969, p. 201, n.4).

13. As witness Keynes' statement in this preface to the French edition of the *General Theory* that "the following analysis [of money and prices] registers my final escape from the confusions of the Quantity Theory, which once entangled me" (*GT* p. xxxiv).

14. Cf. Winch (1969), chaps. 6–8, Stein (1969), chap. 2, 7, Hutchison (1953), chap. 24; (1968), appendix, and Davis (1971). See also Patinkin (1969), pp. 96–98; (1974), pp. 5–7. This point too is further discussed in Chapter 12 below.

I feel that the major revolution effected by the *General Theory* was in the field of theory, and not of policy. And if (unlike the *General Theory*) the *Treatise* did deal at length with policy, it was not because it made any basic, new contribution to this issue, but because it was—as its name indicated—a comprehensive treatise, designed, inter alia, to describe the existing state of the science with respect to both theory and practice.

Just as Keynes' trilogy is bound together by a common concern with the problem of unemployment, so is it bound by a common lack of concern with the problem of economic growth. With respect to the *Treatise* and *General Theory*, this omission can well be understood as a "normal" characteristic of the economic literature of the depression years. For at a time when a dismaying percentage of the existing productive potential was idle, it would have taken an "unrealistic" soul indeed to have concerned himself with the problem of assuring the further growth of this potential. But I think that this lack of concern reflected an additional element in Keynes' thought—and probably in that of many of his contemporaries as well.

In particular, I think that Keynes originally viewed economic growth as a process that would emerge "normally"—and at a satisfactory pace—from a free-market system in which households saved, and then used these savings to purchase the securities which firms issued in order to finance their expansion. "For a hundred years [before World War I] the system worked, throughout Europe, with an extraordinary success and facilitated the growth of wealth on an unprecedented scale" (*Tract*, p. 6)—and Keynes, like his contemporaries, was not much concerned with things outside Europe, in the broad sense of Western civilization.[15] Now, what had seriously interfered with the growth process of Europe after the World War was the disastrous inflations, which had wiped out the real value of past savings and had accordingly discouraged further saving. Correspondingly, a necessary—and sufficient!—condition to reactivate the growth process at a satisfactory pace was to reestablish the confidence of the public in the future real value of its savings (*Tract*, pp. 16–17).

The *General Theory* introduced another factor that interferes with steady growth: unemployment. And parallel to his view in the *Tract*, Keynes felt that once this disturbing factor was eliminated, growth

15. Keynes' *Indian Currency and Finance* (*JMK* I) is not an indication to the contrary: for, as the title of this book indicates, its concern is with the monetary aspects of India; it contains nothing on the "real" side. Indeed, one might almost say that Keynes was not interested in India per se, but in India as a convenient and outstanding example of the workings of a gold-exchange standard.

would again proceed at a satisfactory pace. Indeed, if full employment could be maintained, "a properly run community equipped with modern technical resources, of which the population is not increasing rapidly, ought to be able to bring down the marginal efficiency of capital in equilibrium approximately to zero within a single generation" (*GT* p. 220):[16] the "zero" of the classical stationary state.

In brief, I would conjecture that in Keynes' view at this time there was no need for any special analysis of the process of economic growth. All that one had to do was to ensure the maintenance of two necessary preconditions: a stable value of money and full employment. And growth—to the extent that the economy was still interested in it—would take care of itself.

Another common bond of the *Treatise* and *General Theory*, in quite a different plane, is the fact that the highly novel theoretical developments which mark both works were first presented to the profession at large as finished products, i.e., in the form of published books. In neither case was there any attempt by Keynes to exploit the relatively long period of preparation that was involved (roughly, five years) in order to publish articles in the leading scientific journals on the salient features of his new theories and thus to benefit from the exposure of these theories to the criticism of the profession at large before formulating them in final book form. It is true that such a "research strategy" was much less customary at the time Keynes wrote than it became later.[17] But I would conjecture that Keynes' failure to follow such a strategy also reflected his belief that the quintessence of economic knowledge was concentrated in Cambridge—which geographical point need at most be extended to a triangle that would include London and Oxford.[18] So why bother publishing articles in order to benefit from criticism, if the most fruitful criticisms could be reaped more conveniently and efficiently simply by circulating draft-manuscripts and galley proofs among his colleagues in this fertile triangle?

And as the materials in *JMK* XIII show us, this is indeed the procedure that Keynes employed in the writing of the *General Theory* (see Chapter 7 below). On the other hand—and contrary to the accepted view of the matter—there is little if any evidence that the *Treatise* was subjected to much effective prepublication criticism

16. Cf. also p. 377 of the *General Theory*, where Keynes speaks of accomplishing this aim "within one or two generations."

17. Note that it was also not the "strategy" adopted by Marshall, and this too may have influenced Keynes. See Keynes' 1926 memorial to Marshall as reprinted in his *Essays in Biography* (*JMK* X, pp. 179–80).

18. Cf. Harrod (1951), pp. 322–23.

even within this triangle. And this is particularly true for what Keynes considered to be its major theoretical innovation—the fundamental equations. Correspondingly, there are many serious deficiencies in the *Treatise* which were pointed out immediately after its publication and which (I conjecture) would have been avoided if only it had been subjected to such criticism (see Chapter 3 below). I would also conjecture that it was precisely this unfortunate experience with the *Treatise* that made Keynes so eager to seek out criticism at every stage of the writing of the *General Theory*.

I turn now to some observations on Keynes' style—both analytical and literary. Insofar as the analytical style is concerned, let me start by noting Keynes' failure to make use in his writings of graphical techniques—and this despite the fruitful precedent on this score set by his teacher Marshall,[19] and despite the many passages (especially in the *General Theory*)[20] that almost cry out for the application of such techniques! Here and there in the "trilogy" there are diagrams of a statistical or schematic nature (*Tract*, pp. 83, 87; *TM* I, pp. 290–91; II, p. 317). But in all of these books there is only one diagram of an analytical nature. And even this one exception—which occurs in the course of his discussion of the classical theory of interest—is (as Keynes acknowledges) a diagram that Roy Harrod suggested to him (*GT* p. 180, n.).[21]

Keynes' failure to use graphical techniques in the *General Theory* is even more puzzling in the light of the fact that his chief disciples and critics during the formative period of writing the book—namely, Richard Kahn and Joan Robinson—played a leading role in the breakthrough that was then taking place in the use of such techniques! I am, of course, referring to Joan Robinson's *Economics of Imperfect Competition* (1933), in the writing of which she acknowledged the "constant assistance of Mr. R. F. Kahn" (ibid. p. v). And the puzzle is further increased by the fact (which I have on the authority of Sir Austin Robinson) that Keynes did make use of graphical techniques when lecturing to Cambridge undergraduates.

In connection with Keynes' analytical style, I should also note his oft-cited criticism in the *General Theory* of "symbolic pseudo-

19. I might, however, note that Marshall relegated the analytical diagrams of his *Principles* to the footnotes: he never accorded them equal status with his text.

20. What I particularly have in mind is Keynes' diagramless discussion in Chapter 3 of the determination of the equilibrium volume of employment "at the level given by the intersection of the aggregate demand function with the aggregate supply function" (*GT* p. 30; see also the similar statement on p. 25). This is discussed in detail in Chapter 9 below.

21. For further details, see Chapter 10 below.

mathematical methods of formalising a system of economic analysis
. . . which allow the author to lose sight of the complexities and
interdependencies of the real world in a maze of pretentious and
unhelpful symbols" (*GT* pp. 297–98). We should not, however, uncritically accept this statement as if it were an expression of Keynes'
consistent and unequivocal rejection of mathematical methods. First
of all, Keynes' own analysis in the *Treatise* was in fact largely based
on fairly mechanical applications of the pseudo-mathematical "fundamental equations" (see Chapter 6 below). Furthermore, the
Treatise devoted an entire chapter (20) to "An Exercise in the Pure
Theory of the Credit Cycle," in which Keynes explored in a very
formalistic manner—and under a variety of alternative assumptions—the mathematical properties of his model of the cycle.

Indeed, it may have been Keynes' lack of success with such formal model building in the *Treatise* (see Chapter 7 below) that led him
to the more critical attitude expressed in the passage from the *General Theory* just cited. In any event, it is significant that in the *General Theory*—in contrast with the *Treatise*—Keynes did not attempt
to provide a formal mathematical statement of the theory of employment that constitutes the major theme of the book. Instead, to the
extent that Keynes made use of mathematical analysis in the *General
Theory*, he did so with respect to such secondary themes as the relationship between the own-rates of interest of different goods (Chapter
17, Section II) and the theory of prices (Chapter 21, Section VI). And
even in these instances, the mathematical formulation adds little to
Keynes' literary exposition, and so could be deleted without much
loss of continuity.

Actually, I think it fair to say that the *General Theory* reveals an
ambivalent attitude toward the role of mathematical analysis in
economics; for with all his reservations about the usefulness of such
analysis, Keynes could not resist the temptation to show that he too
could employ it. Thus the quotation from the *General Theory* so
critical of mathematical analysis with which I began this discussion,
actually occurs in Section III of the same Chapter 21 that I have just
cited as providing an instance of the use of such analysis—and indeed
this quotation appears as part of Keynes' apologia for nevertheless
going ahead and resorting to it in Section VI of that chapter! Thus
when all is said and done, I strongly suspect that a comparison of the
General Theory (and a fortiori the *Treatise*) with other works on
economic theory that were written during that period would actually
show Keynes' works to be among the more mathematical of them.

On the other hand, judging from the critical literature that subsequently grew up around Chapters 17 and 21, I think it fair to say that

the mathematical analysis that appears in these chapters is not only not essential to the argument but is also problematic. And this fact —together with the ineffectualness of the "fundamental equations" of the *Treatise*—makes it clear that whatever may have been Keynes' attitude toward the proper role of mathematical methods in economic analysis, his strength did not lie in the use of such methods.

Nor in general did Keynes' analytical strength lie in rigor and precision. Thus in both the *Treatise* and the *General Theory* Keynes frequently failed to specify the exact nature of the assumptions that underlay his argument. Furthermore, as we shall see, there are many ambiguities in these books. And the best evidence of the existence of such ambiguities and obscurities is the fact that forty years later disagreements continue to go on in the literature about the role played in the *General Theory* by such crucial assumptions as wage rigidities, the "liquidity trap," the interest elasticity of investment, unemployment equilibrium, and the like—not to speak of the protracted exegetical debate about the meaning of Keynes' aggregate supply function (see Chapters 9–11 below).

Instead, Keynes' analytical strength lay in his creative insights about fundamental problems that led him to make major "breakthroughs," leaving for those that followed him to correct, formalize, and complete his initial achievements. In the *Treatise*, Keynes thought (erroneously, as it turned out) that his "fundamental equations" constituted such a breakthrough. In the *General Theory*, he saw his breakthrough as lying in his theory of effective demand—and this time he was undeniably right (see Chapters 8–9 below).

In view of this basic aspect of Keynes' analytical style, I should in all fairness also emphasize that the aforementioned lack of rigor and completeness in part reflects the "natural" deficiency of many a pathbreaking work. As Keynes wrote to Joan Robinson: "My own general reaction to criticisms always is that of course my treatment is obscure and sometimes inaccurate, and always incomplete, since I was tackling completely unfamiliar ground, and had not got my own mind by any means clear on all sorts of points" (*JMK* XIII, p. 270). Keynes made this comment in 1932 with reference to the *Treatise*; it is even more relevant for the *General Theory*.

Another characteristic of Keynes' style that should be noted is his constant striving to present the conclusions of his analysis in the form of paradoxes. Sometimes this is very effective, as in the case of the "paradox of saving" in the *General Theory*. Sometimes, however, Keynes' love for the paradoxical tempts him into extreme statements that do not stand up under critical scrutiny, as in the case of the paradox of the widow's cruse in the *Treatise*. And sometimes it tempts him into cryptic statements over whose meaning we continue to puzzle to this very day, such as the oft-cited contention that "there may exist no expedient by which labour as a whole can reduce its *real* wage to a given figure by making revised *money* bargains with entrepreneurs" (*GT* p. 13, italics in original; see below, pp. 55 and 105).

Such obscurities, as well as those mentioned above, frequently impede the flow of the reading. But despite these difficulties, there are constant reminders throughout the trilogy that we are in the presence of a master of English style. The language is generally rich and incisive, enhanced occasionally by well-turned phrases and apt literary allusions. For Keynes' objective is to appeal not only to the intellect but also to the esthetic senses.

This is particularly true of the *Tract*, and for two related reasons: because it is the least technical of the three books and because of its origin as a series of articles on current policy in the *Manchester Guardian*, where Keynes could give full expression to his brilliant publicist style.

Least enjoyable as a reading experience is the *Treatise*, whose generally heavy and constrained style reflects the stately scientific objective that Keynes set for himself in it. Indeed, when one reads the *Treatise* against the background of Keynes' other writings, one cannot escape the feeling that it represents a Keynes out of character, a Keynes attempting to act the role of a Professor, and a Germanic one at that.[22]

In the *General Theory* we once again find the true Keynes. Here (as in so many of Keynes' writings) is the stirring voice of a prophet who has seen a new truth and who is convinced that it—and only it—can save a world deep in the throes of crisis. It is a sharp, polemical voice directed at converting economists all over the world to the new dispensation and combating the false prophets among them who

---

22. Among Keynes' economic writings, the only other one which is similar to the *Treatise* in its relatively dry academic style is his *Indian Currency and Finance* (1913, *JMK* I), which is very much like a Ph.D. thesis—though from the viewpoint of both its scope and the stage of Keynes' career at which it was written, more like a Scandinavian one. Outside of Keynes' economic writings, one should also mention in this context his *Treatise on Probability* (1921, *JMK* VIII) which originated in the fellowship dissertation that Keynes wrote during the period 1906–1909.

In general, it would be worth while studying the intellectual interrelationships between the *Treatise on Probability* and Keynes' economic writings, with particular emphasis on (i) Keynes' theory of the formulation of expectations under uncertainty, (ii) his use of mathematical techniques, and (iii) his views on the applicability of correlation analysis to economic data. In connection with (iii), note Keynes' implicit reference to *The Treatise on Probability* (so I interpret his reference to "thirty years ago") in his 1939 critique of Tinbergen's work (*JMK* XIV, p. 315, last paragraph).

perversely continue with the erroneous teachings of the earlier gods whom Keynes had already abandoned.

And so it is that these writings of Keynes are famous not only for their basic scientific contributions but also for having become part of the literary heritage of every economist. For who does not know that "in the long run we are all dead" (*Tract*, p. 65)? Or that "the ideas of economists and political philosophers, both when they are right and when they are wrong, are more powerful than is commonly understood. Indeed the world is ruled by little else. Practical men, who believe themselves to be quite exempt from any intellectual influences, are usually the slaves of some defunct economist. Madmen in authority, who hear voices in the air, are distilling their frenzy from some academic scribbler of a few years back. . . . The power of vested interests is vastly exaggerated compared with the gradual encroachment of ideas" (*GT* p. 383).

Let me conclude this discussion of similarities and differences among the volumes of the trilogy with a few observations on one additional question: the justification for reading these volumes today. From the substantive viewpoint, all of these volumes are now in the domain of the history of monetary doctrine: their basic scientific contributions have long since been incorporated in the current macroeconomic literature, so that, by definition, the volumes themselves are of importance only to students of this history.

From a broader viewpoint, however, there are sharp differences between these volumes. Thus, in these times of worldwide inflation I think that one can still read with both pleasure and profit Keynes' brilliant discussion of this problem in the *Tract*. On the other hand, the recent revival of interest in the *Treatise* notwithstanding, I can (from the viewpoint of macroeconomic theory) see little profit (and certainly no pleasure) in reading it today. Indeed, my rereading of it now has only convinced me that the hitherto generally accepted view that it is not a good book is fully justified. Nor do I think that the *Treatise* is important as a key to an understanding of the major innovation of the *General Theory*, namely, the theory of effective demand. What the *Treatise* does help us understand is certain terminological peculiarities of Keynes' presentation of this theory; but it contributes little toward an understanding of the substance of the theory itself, which differs so fundamentally from that of the *Treatise*.

As for the *General Theory*, this is the book that made the revolution which has continued to mold our basic ways of thinking about macroeconomic problems. And so the reading of it—at least in part —is an intellectual experience that no aspiring economist even today can afford to forgo.

3.   From the *Tract* to the *Treatise*

It is a familiar fact that the monetary theory that Keynes presented in the *Tract* (pp. 61–70) is, aside from the already noted penetrating analysis of inflation, simply a recapitulation of the cash-
balance approach to the quantity theory developed by his teachers
Marshall and Pigou, on whose writings Keynes explicitly bases his
exposition. Thus Keynes presents the "famous quantity theory of
money" in the following terms:

> Let us assume that the public, including the business world, find
> it convenient to keep the equivalent of k consumption units[1] in
> cash and of a further k' available at their banks against cheques,
> and that the banks keep in cash a proportion r of their potential
> liabilities (k') to the public. Our equation then becomes
>
> $$n = p(k + rk').$$
>
> So long as k, k', and r remain unchanged, we have the same
> result as before, namely, that n and p rise and fall together
> [*Tract*, p. 63].

And this equation is nothing but a minor variation on the famous
"Cambridge equation" that Pigou had first presented in print in his
classic 1917 article (p. 166), to which Keynes at this point refers.

Similarly, when he goes on to explain the determinants of k and k',
Keynes states that "the matter cannot be summed up better than in
the words of Dr. Marshall:

> 'In every state of society there is some fraction of their income
> which people find it worth while to keep in the form of currency;
> it may be a fifth, or a tenth, or a twentieth. A large command of
> resources in the form of currency renders their business easy and
> smooth, and puts them at an advantage in bargaining; but on the
> other hand it locks up in a barren form resources that might yield
> an income of gratification if invested, say, in extra furniture; or a
> money income, if invested in extra machinery or cattle.' A man
> fixes the appropriate fraction 'after balancing one against

---

1. This word has been inadvertently omitted from the new edition.

another the advantages of a further ready command, and the disadvantages of putting more of his resources into a form in which they yield him no direct income or other benefit.' 'Let us suppose that the inhabitants of a country, taken one with another (and including therefore all varieties of character and of occupation), find it just worth their while to keep by them on the average ready purchasing power to the extent of a tenth part of their annual income, together with a fiftieth part of their property; then the aggregate value of the currency of the country will tend to be equal to the sum of these amounts' '' [*Tract*, p. 64].

The words are from Marshall's *Money, Credit, and Commerce* (1923), pp. 44–45. In this source, however, Marshall indicates that in large part they go back to his testimony before the Indian Currency Committee in 1899.[2]

The foregoing passage provides the clear beginnings of an optimum-portfolio approach to the theory of money. Let me however emphasize that it is only a beginning. For Marshall's discussions here and elsewhere in his writings lack one of the basic ingredients of such an approach—namely, a sharp and systematic distinction between stocks and flows, and (correlatively) between wealth and income. This is obvious from the passage that has just been cited: for at one and the same time it describes the people's demand for money as "a fraction of their income" and as "a tenth part of their annual income, together with a fiftieth part of their property." And the fact that Keynes of the *Tract* could uncritically reproduce two such different descriptions of the demand for money shows that at the time he too did not fully recognize the significance in this context of the distinction between wealth and income. Indeed, Keynes himself was more or less to admit this later in the *Treatise* (see below, pp. 41–42).[3]

Within less than a year after the appearance of the *Tract*, Keynes (as Moggridge tells us, *JMK* XIII, p. 15) began working on what was to become the *Treatise*. Unfortunately little survives of these early stages of this work "beyond an extensive collection of draft tables of contents" (ibid.). From these it would appear that the *Treatise*[4] was

2. See this testimony as reproduced in Marshall's *Official Papers* (1926), esp. pp. 267–69. See also Eshag (1963).

3. On the origins of Marshall's two descriptions of the demand for money, see my "Keynesian Monetary Theory and the Cambridge School" (1974), pp. 11–14, 22–23. This article also cites other instances of the failure of Marshall and Keynes of the *Tract* really to apply the portfolio approach to the demand for money.

4. The first table of contents that bears this title is dated June 1927 (*JMK* XIII, p. 47). The original title (from July 1924) was "The Standard of Value" (ibid., p. 15), which after a few variations became (in June 1925) "The Theory of Money and Credit"

originally conceived only as a systemization and elaboration of the theory that lay behind the policy recommendations of the *Tract*, which had not been systematically developed there. Thus in the "Summary of the Author's Theory" that Keynes prepared in November 1924, he presented a conclusion about the determinants of price movements which (in his words) "is the same, though in different words, as the leading tenet of my *Tract on Monetary Reform*" (*JMK* XIII, p. 21).

In the course of his subsequent work on the *Treatise*, however, Keynes greatly expanded its scope. This together with the revisions that he continued to carry out caused the repeated postponement of its publication, which was first planned for 1927, but then deferred to 1929. By August 1929 a one-volume version of the *Treatise* was indeed largely ready in galley and page proof; but then Keynes (to paraphrase his letter to his publisher at that time) felt that he had to "embark upon a somewhat drastic rewriting"—and publication was further delayed until October 1930.[5]

What was the nature of these and earlier revisions? Unfortunately, as already indicated, the materials that would enable us to give a detailed answer to this question have for the most part not survived. There are, however, some observations that can be made. Thus the few extant fragments of the late 1924 draft would seem to suggest that the role of working capital was relatively more important in the early versions of the *Treatise* than in the final one (see *JMK* XIII, pp. 18–24). From Keynes' later correspondence with Robertson it also seems likely that the early versions were based on the view that an excess of investment over saving was necessarily connected with an expansion of the deposits of the banking system—a view which the final version of the *Treatise* was explicitly to negate.

Finally, and most important of all, the early versions of the *Treatise* did not contain what Keynes was later to regard as its major theoretical innovation and as the cornerstone of its analytical edifice—namely, "the fundamental equations" (see Chapter 4 below). True, a reference to such equations had appeared already in the table of contents dated April 1925 (*JMK* XIII, p. 28, title of Chapter 4). But I think it unlikely that this was actually a reference to the fundamental equations in the form in which they finally appeared in the *Treatise*. For the distinctive feature of these equations is their dependence on

(ibid., p. 41). I might note that the draft dated August 1926 bears this title—with "A Treatise on Money" written in the top right corner (ibid., p. 45). I suspect that this was written in after August 1926.

5. This paragraph is based on the materials in *JMK* XIII, pp. 43, 51, 82–83, and 117–18. See also the "Editorial Foreword" to the *Treatise* (I, pp. xiv–xvi).

the difference between savings and investment, and the question of this difference does not seem to have been referred to until the draft table of contents of October 1928 (*JMK* XIII, p. 79, title of Chapter 11). Thus what Keynes probably had in mind when he referred in the earlier draft tables of contents to "fundamental equations" was the various forms of the quantity equation (namely, those of Pigou and Fisher, as well as of Keynes himself in the *Tract*). And lest this be rejected out of hand as an unfounded conjecture, let me note that the *Treatise* as published does indeed refer to these quantity equations as "Alternative Forms of the Fundamental Equations" (title of Chapter 14).

I might in this context also note Frank Ramsey's comment (in a letter he wrote to Keynes after spending a week end with him in August 1928) about "how exciting your quantity equation seemed; I wish I was sufficiently used to thinking about banking to appreciate it fully and to make better criticisms. But I could see that it was a great advance" (*JMK* XIII, p. 78). This may well have been a reference to Keynes' new fundamental equations.

I am afraid that this is the most that we can learn from the materials in *JMK* XIII about the exact period of time during which Keynes first formulated the fundamental equations of the *Treatise*. Fortunately, however, the foregoing conjecture that this occurred during the second half of 1928 is reinforced by Austin Robinson's statement in his memoir on Keynes that "the fundamental equations of the *Treatise* appeared for the first time, I understand, in Keynes' lectures of 1928–9" (E.A.G. Robinson 1947, p. 53).

What was it that stimulated Keynes to make the foregoing revisions and developments? To what extent was it the "natural" result of his own continuous rethinking of the argument, and to what extent was this rethinking further stimulated by criticisms that he may have received of the earlier drafts of the *Treatise*? Once again, we do not have the materials that might enable us to give precise answers to these questions. It is, however, usually thought that the *Treatise* underwent the same kind of intensive prepublication criticism and discussion that the *General Theory* was later to undergo. Thus in the Preface to the *Treatise* Keynes tells us how much he owes "to the atmosphere of discussion and conversation in which I have worked in Cambridge" (*TM* I, p. xviii). And the dust jacket of the present edition of the *Treatise* describes it as "the outcome of six years of intensive work and argument with D. H. Robertson, R. G. Hawtrey and others."

I must, however, express my doubts as to whether this was actually the case. Let me start with one simple indication: there are only

twenty-odd pages of prepublication discussions of the *Treatise* reproduced in *JMK* XIII (pp. 24–26, 117–26, 130–39), as compared with the
voluminous discussions of this kind reproduced in connection with
almost every stage of the writing of the *General Theory*. Furthermore,
most of the aforementioned discussions of the *Treatise* relate to the
last year before its publication and thus may have taken place at too
late a stage to have affected the final result.

Of course, it is possible that there were prepublication discussions
of the *Treatise* which did not survive to be reproduced in *JMK* XIII,
just as the earlier drafts of this book, as well as part of the correspondence relating to them, have for the most part not survived (*JMK*
XIII, pp. 22, 43, 82–83). But even if there were such now missing
discussions, it is quite unlikely that they included important discussions with Keynes' two major critics at the time, Robertson and Hawtrey. It is true that in the Preface to the *Treatise*, Keynes did implicitly refer to discussions with Robertson when he thanked him for
casting "a penetrating light on certain fundamental matters" (*TM* I, p.
xviii). But I suspect that the reference here was to discussions that
had taken place at the earlier stages of the work on the *Treatise*; that
is, before the end of 1928, when (as argued above) Keynes first formulated the analysis of the *Treatise* in terms of the fundamental equations. In any event, it is clear from Robertson's letter of January 1931
that he had not carefully examined Books III and IV of the *Treatise*
before their publication (*JMK* XIII, p. 202); and it is these Books
—with their development of the fundamental equations—that con-
stitute the basic analytical novelty of the *Treatise*.

Further evidence of the fact that Keynes had not really discussed
the final form of the *Treatise* with Robertson before its publication is
provided by a letter that Keynes wrote to him a year after the appearance of the *Treatise*, but which he never sent. In this letter Keynes
explained that the difference of opinion between them about the
analysis of the *Treatise* arose from the fact that Robertson had continued

> with the view you always used to hold, and which I myself held
> up to a moderately late date. When you were writing your *Bank-
> ing Policy and the Price Level* [1926], and we were discussing it,
> we both believed that inequalities between saving and
> investment—using those terms with the degree of vagueness with
> which we used them at that date—only arose as a result of what
> one might call an act of inflation or deflation on the part of the
> banking system. I worked on this basis for quite a time, but in the

end I came to the conclusion that it would not do. . . . My theory as I have ultimately expressed it is the result of this change of view, and I am sure that the differences between me and you are due to the fact that you in substance still hold the old view [*JMK* XIII, p. 273].

And in the *Treatise*, the conclusion to which Keynes refers in this quotation is one of the novel ones that he was at pains to draw from his fundamental equations (*TM* I, pp. 132–33). Surely, then, this basic difference of opinion about the theory finally presented in the *Treatise* would have been discussed by Keynes and Robertson before its publication—if indeed any such discussion had effectively taken place.[6]

In addition to this textual evidence, there are some simple facts of time and space that precluded discussion between Keynes and Robertson during part of the period that the *Treatise* was being written. In particular, from the summer of 1925 to early 1926, Keynes' work on the *Treatise* was interrupted by his marriage and subsequent trip to Russia, as well as by other activities (*JMK* XIII, p. 43). Then, shortly after Keynes returned to work on his manuscript in the spring of 1926, Robertson went off for an eight-month trip to the Far East, from which he did not return until sometime in 1927.[7] And it may well be that the once close collaboration between the two men was never completely resumed after this prolonged interruption.

Insofar as Hawtrey is concerned, it is noteworthy that his most detailed comments were made only a few months before the publication of the *Treatise* in October 1930. Furthermore, they were replied to by Keynes only after the book appeared (*JMK* XIII, pp. 132, 139

6. I am fully aware of the fact that after the appearance of the *General Theory* Robertson continued to argue with Keynes even about points that they had discussed at length before its appearance. But the tone of Keynes' letter here, as well as the general tone of the correspondence between Keynes and Robertson at this time, seems to indicate that this was the first time they were really discussing these basic aspects of the *Treatise* (*JMK* XIII, pp. 271–75; see also pp. 202, 211–12, and 224–31). Supporting evidence for the view in the text is provided by Hicks's statement in his memoir on Robertson that "it is clear that when Robertson had it [i.e., the *Treatise*], he found it less congenial than he had expected at the time when he wrote the preface to *Money* (1928)" (Hicks 1966, p. 15). Cf. also in this connection Robertson's description in his Preface to the 1949 reprint of *Banking Policy and the Price Level* (pp. x–xii) of the changes that took place in Keynes' views from the time of their joint discussions that had originally led up to the analysis of this book until the time that Keynes published the *Treatise*.

7. I am indebted to Sir John Hicks for bringing this fact to my attention; see also Hicks (1966), p. 17.

ff). Keynes apologized for this delay by explaining that he had been " 'overwhelmed' with work with the Macmillan Committee, the Economic Advisory Council 'and a hundred other matters' " (*JMK* XIII, p. 133).

To summarize, in contrast with the *General Theory*, there is little if any evidence that the *Treatise* was subjected to much effective prepublication criticism, and this is particularly true for what Keynes considered to be its major theoretical innovation, the fundamental equations.[8] Furthermore, I think that the absence of such criticism was one of the major reasons that the *Treatise* was not a successful book. But I am getting ahead of the story.

8. Once again, supporting evidence for this conclusion can be found in Austin Robinson's memoir on Keynes, which states: "The fundamental equations of the *Treatise* . . . were still relatively new and relatively undigested even by the people in Cambridge in closest touch with his work when the *Treatise* appeared in 1930" (E.A.G. Robinson 1947, p. 53).

4. The theoretical framework of the *Treatise*: the fundamental equations

One of the standard tasks with which every student of Keynes' writings is confronted is that of tracing the intellectual relationship between the *General Theory* and the *Treatise*. The *Treatise*, however, is a book with strange and forbidding formulas, and even stranger concepts. As a consequence, economists who did their graduate training after the appearance of the *General Theory*—that is, the vast majority of professional economists today—are unlikely ever to have studied the *Treatise* systematically. It will, accordingly, be worthwhile to present a brief summary of the theoretical framework of this book. Since, however, my major purpose is to provide a basis of comparison with the *General Theory*, I shall restrict this summary to the case of a closed economy, the type of economy which was Keynes' almost sole concern in the *General Theory*. This should not cause us to lose sight of the fact that the actual concern of the *Treatise* itself was with the analysis of open economies and, correspondingly, of the international monetary relations that exist among them.

The basic problem that Keynes set out to analyze in the *Treatise* was that of the "credit cycle" and the fluctuations in employment and output which characterize it. His analysis was basically a simple one: profits—by which Keynes means profits above those representing a normal return on capital—are the motive force of the economy (*TM* I, pp. 126, 163). The existence of profits causes firms to expand their respective outputs and hence their demands for the inputs of productive services—and conversely for losses. Now (in the Marshallian terms that Keynes used), profits are the difference between the "demand price" (i.e., market price) of a unit output and its "supply price" (i.e., cost of production). Hence the study of cyclical movements of output reduces to a study of the causes of the differential movements of prices and costs.

It is these movements that Keynes then tries to analyze rigorously by means of his "fundamental equations of prices." These are derived (in Chapter 10 of the *Treatise*) after first distinguishing between "consumption goods" and "investment goods" and then defining the following basic variables of the analysis, where all variables refer to *total* or *aggregate* quantities:

E = current money income = factor earnings = costs of production; *all exclusive of abnormal profits*;

O = the same, at base-period prices;

I' = that part of E earned in the investment-goods sector = current money costs of producing investment goods;

C = the same, at base-period prices;

I = the same, at current market prices, i.e., the current market value of investment goods produced;

$E - I'$ = that part of E earned in the consumption-goods sector = current money costs of producing consumption goods; and

R = the same, at base-period prices.

Keynes then proceeds to define the price variables;

P = current price level of consumption goods;

P' = the same, for investment goods; and

$\prod$ = the same, for output as a whole = the weighted average of P and P'.

Keynes implicitly (and sometimes explicitly) assumes that the base period is one of equilibrium—defined as a situation in which per-unit price = per-unit costs in both the consumption-goods and investment-goods sectors. Hence there is no difference between evaluating current output at base-period prices and evaluating it at base-period costs of production. He then defines what are effectively (1) an index of the money wage rate, W (which rate represents the price of a unit of factors-of-production-in-general) and (2) an index of output per worker, e (or the "coefficient of efficiency"); and he (implicitly)[1] assumes that both of these indexes change in exactly the same way in both sectors. From these definitions it then follows that the change in the cost of production with respect to the base period in both the consumption and investment sectors is

$$\frac{E}{O} = \frac{W}{e} = W_1,$$

where W_1 (which Keynes calls "the rate of efficiency earnings") is accordingly an index of costs of production per unit of output.

From all this, Keynes then derives his two fundamental equations in the following alternative forms:

1. The implicit presence of this assumption was pointed out by Alvin Hansen (1931) in a note to which Keynes replied. Both note and reply have been reproduced as Appendix 2 to Vol. I of the new edition of the *Treatise*.

$$\text{(i)} \quad P = \frac{E}{O} + \frac{Q_1}{R} = \frac{W}{e} + \frac{Q_1}{R} = W_1 + \frac{Q_1}{R}$$

and

$$\text{(ii)} \quad \Pi = \frac{E}{O} + \frac{Q}{O} = \frac{W}{e} + \frac{Q}{O} = W_1 + \frac{Q}{Q}$$

where Q_1 and Q represent profits in the consumption sector and in the economy as a whole, respectively. Thus all that fundamental equation (i) consists of is the quite obvious statement that the change (with respect to the base period) in the price of consumption goods equals the change in the per-unit costs of production of these goods plus the change in per-unit profits (assumed zero in the base period); and equation (ii) makes a correspondingly obvious statement for output as a whole.

The deeper meaning that Keynes attributed to these equations stemmed from his demonstration that profits Q_1 and Q were related to savings and investment. In particular, he first defined current savings S as the difference between income (defined, it will be recalled, as exclusive of abnormal profits) and consumption, or

$$S = E - PR,$$

where all variables are defined in current money terms.

From this definition and those listed earlier in this chapter, it follows that profits in the consumption sector are

$$Q_1 = PR - (E - I') = I' - S,$$

whereas total profits in the economy are

$$Q = (PR + I) - E = I - S.$$

Thus the fundamental equations can be written as

$$\text{(i)}' \quad P = \frac{E}{O} + \frac{I' - S}{R}$$

and

$$\text{(ii)}' \quad \Pi = \frac{E}{O} + \frac{I - S}{O}$$

—and this, indeed, is their primary form[2] in the *Treatise* (I, pp. 122–23). In this way the change in price levels—which for Keynes of

2. From which form Keynes then derives the alternative forms of the fundamental equations presented in (i) and (ii), above. For simplicity, however, I have here reversed the order of derivation.

the *Treatise* was the central concern of monetary theory—was directly related to the excess of investment over savings.[3]

Keynes was fully aware of the triviality of these conclusions per se. In his words:

> These conclusions are, of course, obvious and may serve to remind us that all these equations are purely formal; they are mere identities, truisms which tell us nothing in themselves. In this respect they resemble all other versions of the quantity theory of money. Their only point is to analyse and arrange our material in what will turn out to be a useful way for tracing cause and effect, when we have vitalised them by the introduction of extraneous facts from the actual world [*TM* I, p. 125; see also p. 120].

The specific cause-and-effect relationship that Keynes introduced "from the actual world"—and the one to which he assigned a crucial role in his theory—was that connected with the rate of interest. In particular, a (say) decrease in this rate would cause investment to increase and savings to decrease, thus generate an excess of the former over the latter, thus generate profits, and thus—by the second term of the second fundamental equation—cause prices to rise. In this way, says Keynes, a decrease in the rate of interest would "in itself" cause a price rise—and not only (as in the traditional quantity theory) as the result of its first generating an increase in the quantity of money (*TM* I, pp. 167–76, esp. p. 171).

Keynes also explained the terminology to be used in describing the rate of interest:

> Following Wicksell, it will be convenient to call the rate of interest which would cause the second term of our second fundamental equation to be zero the *natural rate* of interest, and the rate which actually prevails the *market rate* of interest. Thus the natural rate of interest is the rate at which saving and the value of investment are exactly balanced, so that the price level of output as a whole (Π) exactly corresponds to the money rate of the efficiency earnings of the factors of production [i.e., to W_1 in equation (ii) above]. Every departure of the market rate from the

3. For other interpretations of the fundamental equations, see Hicks (1967), chap. 11, and Shackle (1967), chap. 13.

I might here note the differing senses of the term "investment" in Keynes' writings. In the *Treatise* (as we have just seen) it denotes the purchase of new capital goods, and this is also its meaning in the *General Theory*; but in the *Tract* it denotes *financial* investment—that is, the purchase of securities (cf. *Tract*, pp. 4–7, 11–12, 16, and elsewhere).

a deviation of m_i from $\bar{m}$ will cause the price level to become out of balance w/

natural rate tends, on the other hand, to set up a disturbance of the price level by causing the second term of the second fundamental equation to depart from zero [*TM* I, p. 139; italics in original].

Another aspect of his fundamental equations to which Keynes attached great importance was the distinction they make between the two components of a price change: that caused by profits in the manner just explained ("profit inflation"), represented by the respective second terms of these equations, and that caused by changes in the cost of production ("income inflation"), represented by their respective first terms. Between these two types of inflation, there exists, however, an integral relationship. In particular, a profit inflation leads firms to expand their output and hence their demand for the inputs of factors of production, hence "induces" an increase in the "money rates of earnings" of these factors (i.e., W in fundamental equations (i) and (ii) above), and thus generates an income inflation. It follows that if there are no "spontaneous" changes in these rates of earnings—and for the most part Keynes was not concerned with such changes (*TM* I, p. 151)—then a necessary and sufficient condition for price stability is that the market rate of interest equal the natural rate.

From this we can see that—first appearances notwithstanding—Keynes' distinction between profit and income inflation does not parallel the current distinction between demand and cost inflation. First of all, as we have just seen, Keynes' income inflation is not a "spontaneous," exogenous labor-union-monopoly phenomenon, but the "induced," endogenous result of the increased demand for factors of production generated by the excess profits. Second, as we shall see, the income inflation need not bring about a corresponding increase in the price level, but in many cases will be offset by a diminution of the profit inflation. Indeed, this offsetting is a crucial component of Keynes' dynamic analysis, which will be described in the next chapter.

Let me now turn to Keynes' analysis of the determination of the price of investment goods P', which he identifies with the price of equity securities.[4] In a somewhat obscure manner (which was later to

4. That is, he implicitly assumes that the ratio between the market value of the equity securities of any firm and the net book value of the firm's assets is always unity. This is the only way I can interpret Keynes' discussion on pp. 127–31 of the *Treatise* I. I should, however, note the different discussion on p. 222, in which Keynes states that "the price of existing securities [does not] depend at all closely over short periods either on the cost of production or on the price of new fixed capital." Since the discussion on pp. 127–31 presumably also refers to the short period (which is the

be criticized by Kahn), Keynes claims that though both P and P' appear in his fundamental equations,[5] "the price level of consumption goods is unequivocally determined, quite irrespective of the price level of investment goods . . . [which] depends . . . on a different set of considerations" (*TM* I, p. 123). In explaining these "considerations," Keynes then developed some of the major features of what was to become the theory of liquidity preference of the *General Theory*. It is, therefore, worthwhile reproducing this discussion at length:

> When a man is deciding what proportion of his money income to save, he is choosing between present consumption and the ownership of wealth. In so far as he decides in favour of consumption, he must necessarily purchase goods—for he cannot consume money. But in so far as he decides in favour of saving, there still remains a further decision for him to make. For he can own wealth by holding it either in the form of money (or the liquid equivalent of money) or in other forms of loan or real capital. This second decision might be conveniently described as the choice . . . between "bank deposits" and "securities."[6]
>
> There is also a further significant difference between the two types of decision. The decision as to the volume of saving, and also the decision relating to the volume of new investment, relate wholly to current activities. But the decision as to holding bank deposits or securities relates, not only to the current increment to the wealth of individuals, but also to the whole block of their existing capital. Indeed, since the current increment is but a trifling proportion of the block of existing wealth, it is but a minor element in the matter.
>
> Now when an individual is more disposed than before to hold his wealth in the form of savings deposits and less disposed to hold it in other forms, this does not mean that he is determined to hold it in the form of savings deposits *at all costs*. It means that he favours savings deposits (for whatever reason) more than be-

---

concern of the fundamental equations), I have no explanation of this inconsistency. One point worth keeping in mind is that the representative security of the *Treatise* is an equity share, whereas that of the *General Theory* is a bond. I shall return to this point below.

5. In the original form that Keynes wrote them: namely, with Π expressed in the second equation as the weighted average of P and P', or $\Pi = (PR + P'C)/O$, from which Keynes then derived equation (ii)', reproduced above (*TM* I, p. 123).

6. In accordance with Keynes' footnote to this sentence, I have deleted here his reference to the alternative choice "between 'hoarding' and 'investing.'" It is also clear from the context here that by "bank deposits" Keynes means savings deposits.

fore at the existing price level of other securities. But his distaste for other securities is not absolute and depends on his expectations of the future return to be obtained from savings deposits and from other securities respectively, which is obviously affected by the price of the latter—and also by the rate of interest allowed on the former. If, therefore, the price level of other securities falls sufficiently, he can be tempted back into them. If, however, the banking system operates in the opposite direction to that of the public and meets the preference of the latter for savings deposits by buying the securities which the public is *less* anxious to hold and creating against them the additional savings deposits which the public is *more* anxious to hold, then there is no need for the price level of investments to fall at all. Thus the change in the relative attractions of savings deposits and securities respectively has to be met either by a fall in the price of securities or by an increase in the supply of savings deposits, or partly by the one and partly by the other. A fall in the price level of securities is therefore an indication that the "bearishness" of the public—as we may conveniently designate, in anticipation of later chapters, an increased preference for savings deposits as against other forms of wealth and a decreased preference for carrying securities with money borrowed from the banks—has been insufficiently offset by the creation of savings deposits by the banking system—or that the "bullishness" of the public has been more than offset by the contraction of savings deposits by the banking system. . . .

. . . we may sum up the matter thus. The price level of investments as a whole, and hence of new investments [i.e., P'], is that price level at which the desire of the public to hold savings deposits is equal to the amount of savings deposits which the banking system is willing and able to create [*TM* I, pp. 127–29; italics in original].

Keynes' reference here to "later chapters" is a reference to the discussion in Chapter 15 of the *Treatise* of the more general case of "two views" or "two opinions," in which the public itself is divided between bulls and bears. Here Keynes explains that bears include

not only those who have sold securities "short," i.e. have sold securities which they do not own, but also those who would normally be holders of securities but prefer for the time being to hold liquid claims on cash in the form of savings deposits. A "bear," that is to say, is one who prefers at the moment to avoid securities and lend cash, and correspondingly a "bull" is one who prefers to hold securities and borrow cash—the former anticipating that securities will fall in cash value and the latter that they will rise [*TM* I, pp. 223–24].

In this case (to which Keynes was to refer back in the *General Theory*, p. 169 n.) the banking system influences the price of securities not only to the extent that it is willing to generate savings deposits by itself buying securities, but also to the extent that it is willing to grant "easy credit" to the bulls (ibid.) and thus "to act as an intermediary between the two [i.e., bulls and bears] by creating bank deposits, not against securities, but against liquid short-term advances" (*TM* I, p. 129; see also pp. 229–30, 239–40).

Among the basic elements of Keynes' later liquidity-preference theory that can be identified in the foregoing passages is first and foremost the sharp distinction between stocks and flows, and the corresponding notion of an asset-demand for savings deposits as an alternative to the other assets in which an individual can consider holding his wealth. Correspondingly, says Keynes, the decision of individuals to hold savings deposits depends primarily on the "whole block of their existing capital," and only to a minor extent on the "current increment" to this capital (see *TM* I, p. 127, quoted above); i.e., it depends on wealth, and not on income. In contrast with the *General Theory*, however, Keynes does not explicitly present a demand function for these deposits, though he does emphasize that the outcome of his analysis of a change in the quantity of savings deposits depends "on the shape of the public's demand curve for savings deposits at different price levels of other securities" (*TM* I, p. 128).

The *Treatise* also differs from the *General Theory* in placing much less emphasis than the latter on the role of uncertainty in determining the demand for savings deposits.[7] Indeed, in his analysis of this demand in the *Treatise*, Keynes did not even make explicit use of the term "uncertainty." On the other hand, he obviously must have taken implicit account of the existence of uncertainty and of its influence on the demand for savings deposits: for the existence of uncertainty with respect to the future prices of securities is a necessary condition for the existence of "two views" with respect to these prices.

Our discussion of Keynes' analysis of the determination of P' has thus led us to a description of his analysis of the demand for savings

7. This contrast has been much emphasized by Shackle (1967, esp. pp. 172–73). See also Chapter 8, n.27, below.

deposits, which is indeed one of the major contributions of the *Treatise*. A related contribution is Keynes' basic distinction between this demand, which corresponds roughly to the demand for speculative balances in the *General Theory*, and the demand for demand deposits (further classified into income and business deposits), which corresponds roughly to the demand for transactions balances in the *General Theory* (*TM* I, pp. 30–32; *GT* pp. 194–95). Insofar as the individual's demand for income deposits is concerned, Keynes continued to analyze it in terms of Pigou's "Cambridge equation," $P = (kR/M)$, or his own equation of the *Tract* (at the opening of Chapter 3 above). But in his Chapter 14, "Alternative Forms of the Fundamental Equations," Keynes had the following criticisms to make of both these equations:

> (i) The introduction of the factor R, the current income of the community, suggests that variation in this is one of the two or three most important direct influences on the demand for cash resources. In the case of the income deposits this seems to me to be true. But the significance of R is much diminished when we are dealing, not with the income deposits in isolation, but with the total deposits. Indeed the chief inconvenience of the "Cambridge" quantity equation really lies in its applying to the total deposits considerations which are primarily relevant only to the income deposits, and in its tackling the problem as though the same sort of considerations which govern the income deposits also govern the total deposits. . . .
>
> (ii) The prominence given to k, namely the proportion of the bank deposits to the community's *income*, is misleading when it is extended beyond the income deposits. The emphasis which this method lays on the point that the amount of real balances held is determined by the comparative advantages of holding resources in cash and in alternative forms, so that a change in k will be attributable to a change in these comparative advantages, is useful and instructive. But "resources" in this connection ought not to be interpreted, as it is interpreted by Professor Pigou, as being identical with current *income* [*TM* I, pp. 207–8; italics in original].

I interpret this criticism as an implicit reference to Keynes' already discussed analysis of the demand for savings deposits as a function of wealth, and not of income (*TM* I, pp. 127–28, quoted on p. 38 above).

In a related manner, Keynes also criticized his equation of the *Tract* for suggesting that the possible causes of a variation of k' were limited to those which can be properly described as a change of habit on the part of the public. This use of language was not formally incorrect; but it is misleading in so far as it is intended to include, for example, a change in the proportions of the total deposits represented by savings deposits, business deposits and income deposits respectively, due to a change in bank rate or in the business situation as a whole. In short, I was applying to the cash deposits, as a whole, conceptions which were only appropriate to the income deposits [*TM* I, p. 200].

In other words, when one extends the analysis of the demand for money beyond money in the form of income deposits, it is also necessary to take account of the influence on this demand of the rate of interest and of the general state of expectations.

My discussion of Keynes' criticism of the Cambridge cash-balance equation concludes with a mystery: the mystery of Keynes' failure to cite in this context the very similar criticism that had been expressed even before the appearance of the *Tract* by another Cambridge man who had actually been one of his early students: namely, Frederick Lavington's criticism in his *English Capital Market* (1921, pp. 29–33). And the fact that there is also no reference to Lavington in any of the materials of *JMK* XIII–XIV only deepens this mystery.[8]

8. Frederick Lavington (1881–1927) began his studies at Cambridge relatively late (in 1908), after eleven years' service in a bank. Together with Dennis Robertson, Hubert Henderson, and others, he was among Keynes' first students at Cambridge (Harrod 1951, p. 145). After taking his degree in 1911, Lavington returned to administrative work, this time in the government. Then in 1918 he returned to Cambridge to begin an academic career. Cf. the obituaries by H[arold] W[right] and C. R. F[ay] (1927). This late start as well as his illness and early death undoubtedly explain in part why his influence on the development of Cambridge monetary thought was less than it might otherwise have been. But I suspect that an at least equally important factor (especially in the case of Keynes) was Lavington's self-effacing personality as reflected in his favorite saying (as reported by Wright): "It's all in Marshall, if you'll only take the trouble to dig it out" (Wright 1927, p. 504). I am indebted to Lord Robbins for the identification of Harold Wright and for the information that he was the author of the Cambridge Economic Handbook on *Population* (1923).

Donald Moggridge has also informed me that the Keynes Papers contain only one letter from Lavington to Keynes, and none in the opposite direction. This letter dates from July 1911, when Lavington had just taken his degree, and is not concerned with matters of economic analysis. Moggridge has also pointed out to me that neither does Lavington refer to Keynes in his (Lavington's) preface to his *Trade Cycle* (1922), though he does refer to other Cambridge personages. In particular, Lavington acknowledges his debt to Marshall, of course, and Pigou, as well as to his former fellow students and then-colleagues at Cambridge, Dennis Robertson and Hubert Henderson. It might, however, be contended that at that time, Keynes, in contrast to Robertson and his *Study of Industrial Fluctuation* (1915), had not yet made any significant scientific contribution to the field.

An indication of the general neglect suffered by Lavington's work is the fact that *The English Capital Market* (1921) was cited only once in the pages of the *Economic Journal* during the decade following its publication. Furthermore, even this one reference was not to Lavington's prescient elaboration of the Cambridge cash-balance theory, but to his statistical estimates of foreign and home investment (Ashley 1924, p. 527, n.3).

If Lavington's *English Capital Market* has since become better known, it is due primarily to the efforts of Dennis Robertson, who cited it in his later debate with Keynes on the theory of interest (Robertson 1937, p. 431; 1940, pp. 16–17). As Sir John Hicks has informed me, Robertson was also the source of Hicks's reference to this book in his seminal paper, ''A Suggestion for Simplifying the Theory of Money'' (1935, p. 14, n.2). In particular, Hicks added this reference after Robertson (who had read an earlier draft of the paper) called his attention to the passage in Lavington's book that bore on the analytical approach which Hicks developed in that paper.

5. The theoretical framework of the *Treatise*: the dynamic analysis, the quantity theory, and Wicksell

In the preceding chapter, I have summarized the main features of Book III of the *Treatise*, entitled "The Fundamental Equations." Let us now see how Keynes goes on in Book IV—"The Dynamics of the Price Level"—to combine these features into an integrated, dynamic theory. In order to illustrate this theory, I shall briefly sketch Keynes' analysis of the effects of an increase in the quantity of money.

This is the analysis set out in Chapter 17 of the *Treatise*. But an essential preamble to this chapter—as well as to all the others of Book IV—is Chapter 15, "The Industrial Circulation and the Financial Circulation," with which Keynes begins Book IV. By "the industrial circulation" Keynes meant (roughly) demand deposits; by "the financial circulation" (again, roughly) savings deposits. These in turn roughly correspond to what were to become the transactions and precautionary-speculative balances of the *General Theory* (pp. 194–96).

The volume of the financial circulation is determined by the considerations that have already been indicated in the preceding chapter with respect to the choice between saving deposits and securities. Insofar as the industrial circulation is concerned, this is determined by the basic relationship $M_1V_1 = E$, where M_1 is the volume of income (demand) deposits, V_1 their velocity of circulation, and E the level of aggregate money income = aggregate money costs of production (or W_1O). In the real world, V_1 is largely determined by institutional factors and hence remains more or less constant in the short run.

Let us now start from an initial position of equilibrium in which, by definition, the market rate of interest equals the natural rate, so that $I = S$. Assume that this equilibrium is disturbed by an increase in the quantity of money. Initially, only part of this increase will be absorbed in the industrial circulation; part will be used to bid up the price of securities, P', thus generating "windfall profits to the producers of *new* investments" (*TM* I, p. 239, italics in original). The rise in P' may also lead to an increase in the financial circulation—if the bears (who do not expect the increase in P' to continue, and who therefore wish to sell securities and increase their saving deposits)

44

prevail over the bulls to an extent greater than that by which the banking system is willing to create deposits of this kind.

At this point let me pause to note that the increase in P' relative to P does not play a systematic role in this dynamic process: a page later, Keynes considers the alternative possibility that P might increase, without P' necessarily changing (TM I, pp. 240–41). Indeed, Keynes' dynamic analysis here holds even for the case in which P and P' increase in the same proportion, so that no change whatsoever occurs in the relative prices of consumption and investment goods.[1]

In addition to all this there is (to continue with Keynes' analysis) the basic fact that the increase in the quantity of money will have increased the reserves of the banks, thus inducing them to lower the rate of interest at which they lend. As a result, entrepreneurs will increase their borrowings in order to finance the undertaking of new projects, so that investments will begin to exceed savings, thus generating excess profits and an increase in the price of output. But as a result of these profits (as well as those generated by the price increases mentioned two paragraphs above), firms will begin to expand their outputs, thus bringing about an increased demand for inputs, hence to an increase in the wage rate and thereby in the per-unit cost of production. That is, $E = W_1 O$ will increase, and with it the need for industrial circulation. This process will continue until money wages have risen sufficiently to eliminate excess profits and until all of the new money has been absorbed in the resulting increased demand for the industrial circulation. In Keynes' words: "This [process] must continue until $(M_1V_1)/O$ has settled down at a higher figure, which is in equilibrium with the new total quantity of money and also with values of P and P' which are enhanced relatively to their old values in a degree corresponding to the amount by which $(M_1V_1)/O$ has been increased" (TM I, p. 241).

This conclusion has the unmistakeable ring of the quantity theory. And indeed Keynes explains that his second fundamental equation can be rewritten as

$$\text{(ii)}''' \; \Pi = \frac{M_1 V_1}{O} + \frac{I - S}{O},$$

1. Nor do changes in the relative price of consumption and investment goods (i.e., of P'/P) seem to play a systematic role in the subsequent chapters of Book IV, "Changes Due to Investment Factors" (Chap. 18) and "An Exercise in the Pure Theory of the Credit Cycle" (Chap. 20). Indeed, this relative price is barely alluded to in these chapters. See also Keynes' earlier statement that "whilst it is not impossible for the two types of price level to be moving in opposite directions, it is more natural to expect them to move in the same direction" (TM I, p. 163), which again fails to specify anything about the movement of P' relative to P.

which in equilibrium (i.e., when $I = S$) reduces to the Fisherine

$$M_1V_1 = \Pi O .$$

Thus (emphasizes Keynes) for the purpose of comparing market equilibrium positions, the traditional quantity theory does indeed remain valid. The purpose of the *Treatise* in this context, however, is, first, to extend this theory to an economy with a developed banking system, and then to analyze the dynamics of the movement from one equilibrium position to another in such an economy. And this is the role of the interest-rate savings-investment mechanism as it manifests itself in the fundamental equations (*TM* I, pp. 120, 131–33, 137–38). Indeed, at the beginning of Volume II of the *Treatise*, Keynes summarizes the dynamic workings of his second fundamental equation by first writing the quantity equation in the form $M_1V' = \Pi O$ and then stating that the purpose of his new theory is to explain how "during the transition from one position of equilibrium to another" the overall velocity of circulation V' deviates upwards or downwards from its normally constant level in accordance with whether $I - S > O$ or $I - S < O$, respectively (*TM* II, pp. 4–5).[2]

The dynamics of the workings of the quantity theory in an economy with a banking system was one of Keynes' earliest theoretical concerns. Not in the *Tract*—which, as explained above, included only an incidental treatment of monetary theory, but in what (to the best of my knowledge) was Keynes' first published writing on monetary theory: his 1911 review of Irving Fisher's *Purchasing Power of Money*. Here Keynes criticized Fisher for having failed to explain (as, Keynes emphasized, Marshall had) how an influx of money affects prices by first augmenting bank reserves, as a result of which "bankers lend more freely; it is this ease of borrowing which *first* induces merchants and speculators to increase their purchases, and it is this increased demand on their part which raises the level of prices" (Keynes 1911, p. 395; italics in original; see also pp. 11–12 above).

In the light of his later discussion in the *Treatise*, it is noteworthy that Keynes did not mention in this review the lowering of the rate of

---

2. In the present edition and in the original one this equation appears as $M'V' = \Pi O$; but since M' is defined as "the volume of the industrial circulation," I have (in order to maintain continuity with the preceding discussion, which in turn makes use of Keynes' notation in Vol. I of the *Treatise* (pp. 134–35, 218)) written the equation as $M_1V' = \Pi O$. I do not know if the appearance of M' instead of M_1 represents a printing error in the original edition or a change in notation on the part of Keynes. In this context I might, however, note that in *Treatise* I (pp. 211–12) Keynes used the expression $M'V'$ in the sense that Fisher had used it in his equation of exchange—which, of course, differs entirely from the sense in which Keynes used it here.

interest occasioned by the augmented bank reserves—even though Marshall (in his evidence before the Gold and Silver Commission in 1887 and before the Indian Committee in 1898, to which Keynes referred in his review) had emphasized this factor (see Marshall 1926, pp. 41, 51–52, 129–30, 174). In contrast, when in the *Treatise* Keynes came to survey the earlier literature on "bank rate policy," he again cited this evidence—and this time recognized that the lowering of the bank rate played "an obvious part" in Marshall's "causal train" (*TM* I, pp. 171–73). Thus having developed in the *Treatise* a theory that assigned a critical role to the rate of interest, Keynes became sensitized to the appearance of this role in earlier writings as well.[3]

Most of all Keynes was aware, even if somewhat grudgingly, that what he was "trying to say is the same at root as what Wicksell was trying to say" (*TM* I, p. 177, n.3). Keynes made this observation with reference to the fact that both he and Wicksell analyzed the effect of a (say) decrease in the rate of interest on the price level via the *direct* influence of such a change in increasing the demand for investment goods. Correspondingly, as noted in the preceding chapter, Keynes made crucial use in his analysis of Wicksell's "market rate"/"natural rate" distinction.

Actually, my impression of the *Treatise* is that Keynes failed to realize—and hence failed to apply—the full meaning of Wicksell's basic distinction between these two rates. In particular, for Wicksell the "natural rate" represented the marginal productivity of capital and hence existed as a separate analytical entity. But the Keynes of the *Treatise* considered the theory of investment—and indeed all discussions of marginal productivity theory—to be outside the terms of reference of a book on monetary theory. Correspondingly, as we can see from the passage quoted in Chapter 4 above (*TM* I, p. 139), the natural rate was in his view not a separate analytical entity, but a certain value of the market rate: namely, that value at which savings and investment were equal. Not that Keynes did not in a general manner associate the rate of interest with the profitability of investment (cf., e.g., *TM* I, p. 254); indeed, this is a notion that goes back at least to Adam Smith. But nowhere does Keynes precisely define (as he was later to do in the *General Theory*) a rate of return on capital; and correspondingly, nowhere does he define the natural rate of interest in terms of this rate of return.[4]

3. Actually, recognition of the role of the rate of interest in this process goes back to the very beginnings of monetary theory; see the references to Hume, Thornton, Ricardo, et al. cited in my *Money, Interest, and Prices*. Supplementary Note J.
4. This omission is also (see pp. 81–82 below) the source of significant differences

One of the manifestations of this omission is that in the analysis of a monetary change that has been summarized at the beginning of this chapter, Keynes—unlike Wicksell—does not explain that since the real amount of capital has not been affected by such a change, the rate of interest in the new equilibrium position will be the same as in the original one. Nor in his Chapter 18 on changes due to investment factors—in which, inter alia, Keynes analyzes the effects of technological discoveries—does he explain what happens to the equilibrium level of the rate of interest as a result of such changes.

This omission may again reflect Keynes' conception of monetary theory at the time he wrote the *Treatise* as a theory restricted to the analysis of the price level—a conception that did not encourage him to deal explicitly with the implications of his argument for the rate of interest per se. Correspondingly, all that Keynes does emphasize in this context is that whereas "monetary disturbances . . . of a quasi-permanent nature" cause the price level to move from one equilibrium level to another, corresponding "investment disturbances" (e.g., technological changes)—unaccompanied by a change in the quantity of money—generate "an oscillation about an approximately unchanged price level" (*TM* I, p. 248).

Keynes not only failed to derive from Wicksell all that he might have, but also failed to see the full extent of the similarity between his *Treatise* and what Wicksell had written. Thus Keynes wrongly criticizes Wicksell for having failed to "bring out" the implication that a continuous inflationary process also involves a continuous rise in the "rate of money earnings" of the factors of production and in the quantity of money (*TM* I, p. 176, n.3)—an implication which Wicksell had in fact duly emphasized.

What is, however, of far greater significance here is the fundamentally similar conceptions that Wicksell and Keynes had of the relation of their respective works to the traditional quantity theory. For, like Keynes, Wicksell had seen the major purpose of his work as being that of extending the quantity theory to an economy with a developed banking system, and of employing the interest-rate mechanism in

---

between the theories of the demand for money holdings developed, respectively, in the *Treatise* and in the *General Theory*. Keynes' failure to integrate his Wicksellian analysis of the rate of interest with Wicksell's theory of capital (which Wicksell in turn had adapted from Böhm-Bawerk) was one of Hayek's major criticisms of the *Treatise* (Hayek 1931, pp. 279ff). Another manifestation of the absence of marginal analysis in the *Treatise* is the fact that Keynes uses his fundamental equations to analyze changes in output and hence employment without ever taking account of the influence of such changes on the marginal productivity of labor, and hence on the value of e (output per worker) in these equations. Once again, this should be contrasted with the analysis of the *General Theory*, esp. Chap. 2.

order to analyze the dynamic process by which a change in the quantity of money in such an economy affects prices. Indeed, this was the whole purpose of Wicksell's famed "cumulative process."[5]

We can thus readily understand why Gunnar Myrdal—at the time, one of the leading young representatives of the Stockholm School—chidingly referred to Keynes' *Treatise* as an example of "the attractive Anglo-Saxon kind of unnecessary originality, which has its roots in certain systematic gaps in the knowledge of the German language on the part of the majority of English economists" (Myrdal [1933] 1939, pp. 8–9).[6] But as one who himself was able to read Wicksell's works only in the English translations which became available after the appearance of the *Treatise*, I am hardly in a position to press this criticism!

5. For detailed documentation from Wicksell's *Interest and Prices* (1898) and *Lectures on Political Economy* (1906) in support of the foregoing interpretation, see my *Money, Interest, and Prices*, Supplementary Note E:4, especially pp. 588–89 and 591–92.

6. Of obvious relevance in this context was Keynes' statement that "in German I can only clearly understand what I know already!—so that *new* ideas are apt to be veiled from me by the difficulties of language" (*TM* I, p. 178, n.2; italics in original).

6. Some further reflections on the fundamental equations

As the name he gave them indicates, Keynes saw in his "fundamental equations of price" the major contribution of his *Treatise*. As he said in his 1931 Harris Lecture: "That is my secret, the clue to the scientific explanation of booms and slumps (and of much else, as I should claim) which I offer you" (*JMK* XIII, p. 354). But the very fact that Keynes was so convinced of the importance of his equations was, I suspect, also the source of some of the major deficiencies of his *Treatise*.

Thus I have suggested on p. 48 that Keynes' overconcentration on the equilibrium price levels determined by these equations may lie behind his failure to explore the implications of his analysis for the equilibrium level of the rate of interest. I also suspect that Keynes' "single-equation approach" was the source of his failure really to combine the component parts of his analysis into an integrated whole. True, the analysis of the *Treatise* (as we have seen in the particular instance of a change in the quantity of money described in the preceding chapter) does assign an important role to the interaction of the price and output developments in the markets for consumption and investment goods with the corresponding developments of the "requirements for the monetary circulation." But though Keynes recognizes in this context that he is "dealing with a case of multiple [i.e., general] equilibrium in which each element affects every other element more or less" (*TM* I, p. 129), he never explicitly supplements his fundamental equations of equilibrium in the markets for goods with an equation that systematically analyzes the achievement of equilibrium between the demand and supply for money. It is as if Keynes' obvious conviction that his fundamental equations were something sui generis left no room in his thinking for any other equations in the system. Correspondingly, the impression one gets from the *Treatise* is that the money market is not an equal partner in determining events; instead, it only places some bounds on the events as determined in the markets for goods.

Keynes (as already quoted in Chapter 4 above) was fully aware that his fundamental equations are "mere identities" and that "their only point is to analyze and arrange our material in what will turn out to be a useful way for tracing cause and effect" (*TM* I, p. 125). Nevertheless, in reading the *Treatise* I have had the uncomfortable feeling that Keynes was so enthusiastic about what he felt were the new truths revealed by his fundamental equations that he all too frequently shifted unawares across the slippery line that lies between "tracing cause and effect" and simply repeating the tautologies inherent in these equations.[1]

Thus, in what sense can one talk about "a fall in the price of consumption goods *due to* an excess of saving over investment" (*TM* I, p. 130; italics added), when savings and investment are *defined* in such a manner that (by the first fundamental equation) the existence of such an excess *means* that this price has fallen?[2] A similar comment can be made with respect to Keynes' reference to "the rigour or the validity of our *conclusions* as to the quantitative effect of divergences between saving and investment on the price levels ruling in the market" (*TM* I, p. 145; italics added). I should note that in part these difficulties stem from Keynes' failure in the *Treatise* (as he himself was later to admit; see page 73 below) to distinguish adequately between planned and actual quantities.[3]

Similarly, all too frequently Keynes translates the symbols of his fundamental equations into words (without always indicating that this is what he is doing) and then treats these translations as if they had more analytical content than the identities which they simply verbalize. And even when this is done in a way which succeeds in escaping the tautologies of the fundamental equations, Keynes' argument at these points reduces to an extremely mechanical application of these equations. The following are examples of what I have in mind.

When for any reason an entrepreneur feels discouraged about the prospects, one or both of two courses may be opened to him—he can reduce his output or he can reduce his costs by lowering his

---

1. In this context I might also mention a letter that Keynes wrote to the Governor of the Bank of England in May 1930 in which he based his argument on the "difficult theoretical proposition" that "if our total investment . . . is less than the amount of our current savings . . . then—in my opinion—it is absolutely certain that business losses and unemployment *must* ensue" (italics in original). Keynes went on to say that it was "very important that a competent decision should be reached whether it [i.e., the proposition] is true or false. I can only say that I am ready to have my head chopped off if it is false!" Cited by Howson and Winch (1976), chap. 3, n.54.

2. Actually, this was one of Hawtrey's criticisms of the proofs of the *Treatise* that Keynes had sent him for his comments a few months before publication. *JMK* XIII, pp. 152 (points 9–10) and 153 (point 13). The first of these passages is quoted in full in Chapter 7, p. 54 below.

3. And on this point, too, Hawtrey had criticized him.

offers to the factors of production. . . . both courses are likely to aggravate their losses by reducing the cost of investment [*TM* I, p. 144].

The last sentence is clearly a translation of the second term of the first fundamental equation, equation (i) of Chapter 4 above. Or consider the following translation of this equation, presented in the guise of a demonstrated proposition:

Our fundamental equation has demonstrated that, if costs of production remain constant, the purchasing power of money [with respect to consumption goods] suffers a seesaw movement up and down according as the volume of savings exceeds the cost of investment or the cost of investment exceeds the volume of savings. On the other hand, if the volume of savings is equal to the cost of investment, then the purchasing power of money fluctuates inversely with the cost of production. . . . We now define the *credit cycle* to mean the alternations of excess and defect in the cost of investment over the volume of saving and the accompanying seesaw in the purchasing power of money due to these alternations [*TM* I, pp. 248–49; italics in original].

Consider again the translation of the first fundamental equation contained in the first two clauses of the following sentence and presented as part of a "proof":

We have claimed to prove in this treatise that the price level of output depends on the level of money incomes relatively to efficiency [i.e., on W/e in equation (i)′ in Chapter 4 above], on the volume of investment (measured in cost of production) relatively to saving, and on the "bearish" or "bullish" sentiment of capitalists relatively to the supply of savings deposits available in the banking system [*TM* II, p. 309].

My major criticism of these passages and many similar ones in the *Treatise* is that even when they are not tautological, they are extremely formalistic and mechanical. Thus they claim that (say) an excess of investment over saving increases the price of goods not because such an excess represents the existence of pressures of excess demand in the market for goods, but because such an excess means that the second term of the second fundamental equation is positive!

This mechanicalness is thus related to another characteristic of the *Treatise*, Keynes' tendency in it to endow the terms of his fundamental equations with an existence of their own. The following passages are good illustrations of what I have in mind.

> We have seen that the price level will have responded to the increased (or decreased) quantity of money as soon as the second term of the fundamental equation is affected [*TM* I, p. 241].
>
> It must not be supposed, however, that this transition from an enhancement of prices as a result of an increase in the second term of the fundamental equation to their enhancement as a result of an increase in the first term will necessarily take place smoothly [*TM* I, p. 242].
>
> When bank rate is raised, not in the interests of equilibrium to keep the second term from rising, but in order to bring the first term down . . . [*TM* I, p. 245].

To me, all this is a further manifestation of the "magic-formula mentality" described at the beginning of this chapter (see also Chapter 12 below).

7. From the *Treatise* to the *General Theory*: criticism and development

From all indications, Keynes originally conceived the *Treatise* as a book that would be recognized for years to come as the definitive work on the pure and applied theory of money. Despite this ambitious goal, the book, at least from the viewpoint of its contribution to pure theory, is not a finished work. I do not say this from the vacuous viewpoint that the *Treatise* does not contain what the *General Theory* was later to contain, but from the viewpoint of the degree of integration and internal consistency of its own theoretical framework, as well as of the validity of its component parts.

In his Preface to the *Treatise* (p. xviii), Keynes himself confessed that it "represents a collection of material rather than a finished work." He attributed this deficiency to the fact that during the writing of the book "my ideas have been developing and changing, with the result that its parts are not all entirely harmonious with one another. The ideas with which I have finished up are widely different from those with which I began. There are many skins which I have sloughed still littering these pages. It follows that I could do it better and much shorter if I were to start over again" (*TM* I, p. xvii).

All this is undoubtedly true. But as indicated in Chapter 3 above, I suspect that an even more important reason for the deficiencies of the *Treatise*, and of its theoretical core in particular, was that it had not been subjected to enough professional criticism before its publication.

Be that as it may, it rapidly became clear to Keynes that some of the central propositions of the *Treatise* could not stand up under critical scrutiny. Thus, shortly before the publication of the *Treatise* in October 1930, Hawtrey had incisively criticized "Mr. Keynes' formula" on the grounds that, on the one hand, it was a tautology, and not (as Keynes would have it) an *explanation* of the price change (see Chapter 6, n.2, above); and that, on the other hand, the "formula only takes account of the reduction of prices in relation to costs, and does not recognize the possibility of a reduction of output being caused directly by a contraction of demand without an intervening fall of price" (*JMK* XIII, p. 152).[1] A few months later came Richard

---

1. This is a quotation from the notes that Hawtrey made on the proofs of the

Kahn's demonstration (*JMK* XIII, pp. 203–7, 219) that Keynes' attempt to make an absolute distinction between the allegedly different ways in which the prices of consumption (*P*) and investment (*P'*) goods were respectively determined simply stemmed from some very special assumptions that he had tacitly made. And the participants in the "Cambridge Circus" (on which more in a moment) demonstrated that the paradox of the widow's cruse that had so delighted Keynes (*TM* I, p. 125) was simply the consequence of his tacit assumption—which contradicted the basic general assumption of the *Treatise*—that despite the existence of profits, output remained constant (*JMK* XIII, p. 339).

I would conjecture that it was this experience that was the major source of Keynes' observation in the Preface to the *General Theory* that "it is astonishing what foolish things one can temporarily believe if one thinks too long alone, particularly in economics (along with the other moral sciences), where it is often impossible to bring one's ideas to a conclusive test either formal or experimental" (*GT*, p. xxiii). So if, as Austin Robinson tells us (E.A.G. Robinson 1947, p. 55), it was a fortunate "coincidence" that there was in the early 1930's "a remarkable younger generation in Cambridge" who could supply criticisms to Keynes as he developed his *General Theory*, I suspect that an equally important part of this fruitful "coincidence" was the fact that—as a result of his unhappy experience with the *Treatise*—Keynes then had a demand for such criticism!

In the process of criticism and development as revealed by the materials of *JMK* XIII, I think we can roughly distinguish three main stages: a first stage of (to borrow Moggridge's term) "arguing out the *Treatise*," which lasted until (say) the end of 1931; a second stage—the crucial, formative stage of writing the *General Theory*—which in part overlapped the first stage and ended (at the latest) with the mid-1934 draft of the book; and a third stage which took up most of 1935 and was devoted to obtaining detailed criticisms of the successive galley proofs of the book. As we shall see from the description which follows, these stages differed not only with respect to their major emphasis but to a certain extent also with respect to the individuals involved.

An integral part in the creative process which produced the *General Theory* was also played by the lectures on monetary economics

---

Treatise that Keynes sent him in the spring and summer of 1930, and to which Keynes did not reply until the end of November 1930. As Moggridge points out (*JMK* XIII, p. 132), these notes eventually appeared in the long critique of the *Treatise* that Hawtrey published as chap. 6 of his *Art of Central Banking* (1932). The passage cited here appears in an elaborated form on pp. 336–38 of that book. See also above, pp. 31–32.

which Keynes continued to give each year at Cambridge during the fall term. In his memoir on Keynes, Austin Robinson has described these lectures as "something wholly unlike anything else that [he had] ever known in Cambridge lectures. Apart from the third-year undergraduates, to whom officially the course was addressed, there were to be found there the whole body of research students, at least half the members of the Faculty, a visiting Professor or two from America, Australia or where you will, and on occasion a few spies . . . from London, Oxford, or elsewhere" (E. A. G. Robinson 1947, p. 56). And from notes on these lectures which have fortunately been preserved (n.11 below), we can see how Keynes used them as a means of expounding and further developing his ideas as his work on the *General Theory* progressed.

To the first stage of the critical process belong the discussions of the famous "Cambridge Circus." This was the name given to the members of the aforementioned "younger generation" (most of whom were then between twenty-five and thirty) who immediately after the publication of the *Treatise* formed a group for the purpose of undertaking a critical examination of the book. The "Circus" included Richard Kahn, James Meade, Piero Sraffa, and Joan and Austin Robinson, with Kahn serving as the channel of communication between Keynes and the group. One of Donald Moggridge's most valuable contributions as editor of *JMK* XIII and XIV is his reconstruction, on the basis of the "pooled memories" of the aforementioned participants, of the major discussions of the "Circus" during the first half of 1931 (*JMK* XIII, pp. 337–43).[2]

During this period, Keynes also continued to "argue out" the *Treatise* with Dennis Robertson—who, though he was at Cambridge, did not wish to be deeply involved in the meetings of the younger people of the "Circus" (*JMK* XIII, p. 338). This discussion ultimately led to an exchange in the pages of the 1931 *Economic Journal* (*JMK* XIII, pp. 219–38)—the first published disagreement between Keynes and Robertson on questions of monetary theory.[3] But what apparently affected Keynes far more deeply[4] was a sharp, two-part critique of the *Treatise* by F. A. Hayek in the pages of *Economica* (1931,

2. See, however, n.8 below.
3. I suspect that the period of close agreement between them on such questions—a period characterized by Robertson's statement in his *Banking Policy and the Price Level* (1926, p. 5) that he did not know "how much of the ideas therein contained is [Keynes'] and how much is mine"—had actually come to an end several years earlier, and certainly before the period (ca. 1928) in which Keynes began to develop the theory of the *Treatise* in its final form; see above, pp. 30–31.
4. To the extent that he even expressed doubts (in a penciled note on the margin of his copy of Hayek's review) about the latter's "good will" (*JMK* XIII, p. 243).

1932), to the first part of which Keynes replied (*JMK* XIII, pp. 243–56). This set off further correspondence with Hayek as well as Robertson and culminated in yet another exchange with the latter in the 1933 *Economic Journal* (*JMK* XIII, pp. 257–330).

On some of the foregoing criticisms there was an immediate and productive meeting of the minds. This was true, for example, of Hayek's complaint about the absence of a theory of capital and interest in the *Treatise*. On this point Keynes conceded (in the reply he published in November 1931) that "later on, I will endeavour to make good this deficiency" (*JMK* XIII, p. 253)—as he of course did in the *General Theory*. Again, in his belated (November 1930) letter of reply to Hawtrey's aforementioned criticism that he had not adequately dealt with changes in output, Keynes continued to insist that "the question *how much* reduction of output is caused, whether by a realised fall of price or an anticipated fall of price, is important, but not strictly a monetary problem" (*JMK* XIII, p. 145, italics in original), but at the same time he admitted (only a month after the appearance of the *Treatise*!):

> If I were to write the book again, I should probably attempt to probe further into the difficulties of [the theory of short-run output]; but I have already probed far enough to know what a complicated affair it is.
>
> As it is I have gone no further than that anticipated windfall loss or profit affects the output of entrepreneurs and their offers to the factors of production; but I have left on one side the question *how much* output is affected and also whether output can be affected in any other way [*JMK* XIII, p. 146; italics in original].

Similarly, there can be no doubt about the invaluable stimulus to Keynes' rethinking of the *Treatise* that was generated at this time by the criticisms along these lines, and others, of the members of the "Cambridge Circus" (*JMK* XIII, pp. 337–43; see also Keynes' letter to Joan Robinson cited at the beginning of the next chapter).

On the other hand, a good deal of the polemics between Keynes, on the one hand, and Robertson, Hayek, and (to a lesser extent) Hawtrey, on the other, was quite unproductive (though I am not at all sure that it was any more unproductive than the polemics that go on today in the journals). There was much talking past each other, as each of the participants remained within his own conceptual framework and thus failed to communicate effectively with the other. In particular (and in this respect, at least, I think the profession has since improved) much of the discussion was devoted to long, tiresome, and inconclusive debates about terminology—and particularly about the "proper" definitions of "saving" and "hoarding."

A typical reaction to such fruitless discussions was, for example, Keynes' remark at the end of his published November 1931 reply to Hayek about "how thick a bank of fog still separates his mind from mine" (*JMK* XIII, p. 256). And though in the correspondence that followed, Keynes continued with his persistent attempts to pin Hayek down on his definition of saving—repeatedly but unavailingly pressing him to "give a formula which shows how saving is *measured*" (*JMK* XIII, p. 257; italics in original)—Keynes, in great frustration, concluded the correspondence in February 1932 with a confession to Sraffa and Kahn "that the abyss yawns," even though he could not "help feeling that there *is* something interesting in it" (*JMK* XIII, p. 265; italics in original).

In any event, as a result of all the foregoing criticism, Keynes, within a remarkably short time after the appearance of the *Treatise*, was already engaged in the basic reexamination of its analysis that was to lead ultimately to the *General Theory*. And the most important aspect of this reexamination was Keynes' recognition of the crucial necessity of developing the theory of short-run output that—as Hawtrey and the various members of the "Cambridge Circus" had emphasized—was missing from the *Treatise*.

The details of this development will be the subject of the next chapter. Let me here note that the first explicit reference that I have been able to find in the documents reproduced in *JMK* XIII that seems to indicate that Keynes had actually begun writing a new book occurs in a letter of reply written in December 1931 to Nicholas Kaldor (then a research student at the London School of Economics) in which Keynes stated that he was "now endeavouring to express the whole thing over again more clearly and from a different angle; and in two years' time I may feel able to publish a revised and complete version" (*JMK* XIII, p. 243). Again, in the spring of 1932, in the Preface to the Japanese edition of the *Treatise* (I, p. xxvii), Keynes announced his intention "to publish a short book of a purely theoretical character, extending and correcting the theoretical basis of my views as set forth in Books III and IV [of the *Treatise*]." Similarly, in a letter written to Ralph Hawtrey in June 1932—in connection with the latter's reprinting of his aforementioned criticism of the *Treatise*[5]—Keynes wrote: "I am working it out all over again" (*JMK* XIII, p. 172).[6]

5. See n.1, above.
6. On this chronology, see Moggridge's "Editorial Introduction" to the *General*

Unfortunately, relatively little material related to this crucial, initial stage of work on the *General Theory* (as distinct from the "arguing out" of the *Treatise*) has survived. That which has (and for which we can only be most grateful) consists almost entirely of drafts of various chapters of the *General Theory* written in 1932 (*JMK* XIII, pp. 381–405) and 1934 (ibid., pp. 423–56, 471–84), respectively. In addition, there are some odd notes and comments on these drafts that Keynes exchanged with Kahn and Joan Robinson, as well as some comments by the latter on the related lectures that Keynes was then giving at Cambridge (*JMK* XIII, pp. 373–80 and 419).[7] It is, however, clear that there must have been many additional oral discussions of these drafts of which there is no record. Thus in March 1934, Keynes wrote Joan Robinson that he was "going through a stiff week's supervision from R. F. K[ahn]. on my M.S." (*JMK* XIII, p. 422). Moggridge also refers to a long visit to Keynes made by Kahn in September 1934 that was again devoted to reviewing parts of the manuscript (*JMK* XIII, p. 484).

As I shall argue in the next chapter, the analytical structure and terminology of the aforementioned 1934 draft are already those that were to characterize the *General Theory* in its published form, so that this draft can be said to mark the end of the formative stage of the writing of this book. Correspondingly—if we are to judge from the material that has survived to be reproduced in *JMK* XIII—the criticisms which influenced Keynes' work during this formative stage emanated almost entirely from his junior colleagues at Cambridge, and from Richard Kahn and Joan Robinson in particular.

What was the nature of the intellectual relationship that developed between Keynes and these colleagues? This type of question is always a very delicate and complicated one—and a fortiori so in the case of as intensive an intellectual interaction as the one that took place here. In this connection Moggridge tells us—on the basis of the "pooled memories" of the major surviving members of the "Circus"—that "there may have been (as some members believe) a short period when the 'Circus' was slightly further on towards the *General Theory* than was Keynes. But it was a very short time"

Theory (pp. xv–xix), as well as his comments on p. 337 of *JMK* XIII, though Moggridge does not refer to the letter to Kaldor. See also Moggridge's illuminating article "From the *Treatise* to the *General Theory*: An Exercise in Chronology" (1973). See also Lambert's "Evolution of Keynes's Thought from the Treatise on Money to the General Theory" (1969).

7. Thus see Joan Robinson's reference to these lectures in her letter from May 1932 reproduced on p. 376 of *JMK* XIII. I should note that Keynes also had some correspondence with Robertson about Keynes' 1932 lectures (*JMK* XIII, pp. 294ff).

(*JMK* XIII, p. 342). This is apparently the minority view of the aforementioned members of the "Circus." I feel, however, that these "memories" have led some of them to claim too much for the "Circus";[8] correspondingly, I tend to agree with the implied majority view. More generally, the description to be presented in the next chapter of the development of the theory of effective demand (which is, after all, the major contribution of the *General Theory*) seems to me clearly to show Keynes in the role of the intellectual innovator, continuously striving for better formulations of the theory of output, and then subjecting these successive formulations to the penetrating and fruitful criticisms of his younger colleagues. In brief, it seems that the relationship between Keynes and the members of the "Circus" was not basically different from the kind of invaluable relationship that frequently evolves between the author of a new work and the close band of sympathetic discussants that he in one way or another selects to criticize and stimulate the early stages of its development.

Be that as it may, it was only after galley proofs of the *General Theory* started to flow in early 1935 that Keynes exposed his work to the criticisms of economists outside the intimate world of his junior colleagues at Cambridge. For this purpose he renewed his correspondence with D.H. Robertson in January 1935 (*JMK* XIII, p. 493), and two months later with Ralph Hawtrey (ibid., p. 565). And a little later again, in June 1935, Keynes also began to send proofs to Roy Harrod at Oxford (ibid., p. 525). Needless to say, these proofs were also circulated to Richard Kahn and Joan Robinson. And almost all of the correspondence reproduced in the chapter of *JMK* XIII entitled "Towards the General Theory" is with these five individuals.

This correspondence, like the earlier one on the *Treatise*, was carried out with great fervor. In more than one instance, letters were delivered the same day they were written—and answered on the spot! This not only reflects the intensity of the discussion, but also arouses

8. Thus in his summary of the discussions of the "Cambridge Circus," Moggridge reports that "James Meade, an active participant in the discussions, returned to Oxford in the autumn of 1931 at the end of his year's visit to Trinity, Cambridge. He is cautiously confident that he took with him back to Oxford most of the essential ingredients of the subsequent system of the *General Theory*" (*JMK* XIII, p. 342). The evidence to be presented in the next chapter, however, indicates that Meade could not at that time have taken back with him that most essential ingredient of all—the theory of effective demand—which was developed only during 1933. Similarly, I have not found support in the materials of *JMK* XIII and XIV for Joan Robinson's recent contention that these volumes show "that there were moments when we had some trouble in getting Maynard to see what the point of his revolution really was, but when he came to sum it up after the book was published [in his 1937 *Quarterly Journal of Economics* article reprinted in *JMK* XIV, pp. 109–23] he got it into focus" (Robinson 1973, p. 3).

ancient memories of the then-famed efficiency of the British postal service![9] And similarly ancient memories—of a time when printing costs were quite different from what they are today—are aroused by the readiness with which Keynes continued to rewrite large parts of the *General Theory* in galley proof. Indeed, he circulated such proofs for critical comments in much the same way that we today circulate mimeographed or photocopied versions of our draft manuscripts!

I have already expressed the opinion that the formative stage of the *General Theory* had been completed by the end of 1934 at the latest. As a corollary, I also think that even though the detailed criticisms of the proofs that stemmed from the aforementioned correspondence were undoubtedly of great value in leading Keynes to clarify the exposition and tighten the argument at various points,[10] they did not for the most part affect the book's basic conceptual framework. The only (partial) exception to this that I have noted is Roy Harrod's largely unsuccessful attempt to get Keynes to take a more general-equilibrium view of his analysis (see Chapter 10 below).

But even in this context of criticisms of detail, we must distinguish between the effective criticisms that continued to be made throughout 1935 by Keynes' younger colleagues (Kahn, Joan Robinson, and Harrod), who had adopted his conceptual framework, and the criticisms made by Keynes' contemporaries (Robertson and Hawtrey), who had not. For in the latter case, the fact that the critics approached the problems being discussed from different conceptual frameworks—and different definitions—once again frequently prevented fruitful communication. Indeed, after long correspondence, Keynes (in March 1935) somewhat testily declared to Robertson that "our minds have not really met," agreed that they "had better break off the discussion at this point," and promised to send Robertson (who should "not feel under any obligation to make any comments") the "page proofs as they came along"—an offer which Robertson politely but firmly (for him!) declined (*JMK* XIII, pp. 520–24). And the breach between them became "official" when, in the Preface to the *General Theory*, Keynes did not even include Robertson's name in his list of acknowledgments to those from whose criticisms he had benefited.

In the case of Hawtrey—whose name is mentioned in the Preface—the long prepublication correspondence (*JMK* XIII, pp. 565–633) was more fruitful. But even here, after stating in November

9. I am referring to intercity mail; thus see the exchange with Hayek—albeit with respect to the *Treatise*—on 25 December 1931 (*JMK* XIII, pp. 259–60).

10. The changes that Keynes made in the successive proofs of the *General Theory* during this period have been carefully and usefully recorded by Moggridge in the long appendix to *JMK* XIV (pp. 351–512).

1935 that "if this correspondence does not fatigue you, there is nothing that I like better," Keynes tired of the correspondence and expressed the opinion (in a letter to Hawtrey from January 1936) that "I have not yet succeeded in some aspects in conveying to you what I am driving at." Indeed, half a year before that, Keynes had already complained to Kahn that "Hawtrey's comments indicate that he hasn't the faintest idea what I'm driving at" (*JMK* XIII, pp. 600, 627, and 634; see also pp. 612–13 and 630–31).[11]

We should not, however, conclude from all this that Robertson and Hawtrey had no influence at all on the final form of the *General Theory*. The question of the extent and nature of this influence is, instead, still an open one that deserves detailed study on the basis of the complete correspondence now made available in *JMK* XIII. Let me here only note, for example, that though we usually remember Keynes' footnote acknowledgment to Roy Harrod for his suggestion of the only analytical diagram that appears in the *General Theory*, we tend to forget that in this footnote Keynes also referred to the "partly similar schematism" that Robertson had used in an article (1934) he published in the *Economic Journal* almost a year before the Keynes-Harrod correspondence on this point (*GT* p. 180 n.; *JMK* XIII, pp. 544–61).

Let me also say that Robertson and Hawtrey were then probably voicing similar complaints to their friends about Keynes' failure to understand them! Correspondingly, I feel that the frequent attempts to place the entire blame for the lack of communication on their shoulders does them an injustice. Thus I shall later note Hawtrey's valid, though unavailing, criticism in the galley-proof stage of

11. In all this, Keynes manifested a most human ambivalence: on the one hand, he despaired of achieving communication; on the other, the polemicist in him could not let go. This same ambivalence prevailed with respect to Pigou—or "the Prof," as he was referred to. As Keynes wrote to Kahn: "the stuff [Pigou] writes seems to me the most extraordinary in some ways in the history of the subject. But it has a dreadful fascination for me, and I cannot leave it alone" (*JMK* XIII, p. 525).

Having myself always had great difficulty in understanding Pigou's writings of the period, I must admit that I draw comfort from the fact that such difficulties also existed for some of Pigou's own colleagues and former students! Thus in addition to Keynes' comment just cited (and he made many other such comments, as can be seen from *JMK* XIII, p. 310, and *JMK* XIV, pp. 234–68, especially pp. 234 and 238), see Gerald Shove's complaint (in his letter of September 1933 to Keynes) that he found it "very difficult to make out what exactly he [Pigou] is saying" in his then new book on *The Theory of Unemployment* (*JMK* XIII, p. 321; see also Kahn's reference to Shove in *JMK* XIV, p. 258). And in a letter that Robertson wrote to Keynes at roughly the same time, even Robertson admitted that he had "always found the Prof's wage-good method hard to get into" (*JMK* XIII, p. 313). Nevertheless, Robertson generally tended to give Pigou a more sympathetic reading, and to defend him accordingly against Keynes' criticisms (*JMK* XIII, pp. 318–19; *JMK* XIV, pp. 251–55).

Keynes' obscure presentation of his theory of effective demand. Similarly, one of Robertson's major criticisms of the proofs that Keynes sent him in February 1935 was that the rate of interest reflects the joint influences of the propensity to save, the productivity of capital, and liquidity preference—and not (as Keynes kept on insisting) of this last influence alone (*JMK* XIII, pp. 499 and 509). And in that debate, it was not Robertson who was the wrongheaded one.

8.   From the *Treatise* to the *General Theory*: the development of the theory of effective demand

What is the major analytical innovation of the *General Theory*, its major differentia from the *Treatise*? The answer which Keynes gave to this question in the Preface to the *General Theory* is as follows:

> When I began to write my *Treatise on Money* I was still moving along the traditional lines of regarding the influence of money as something so to speak separate from the general theory of supply and demand. When I finished it, I had made some progress towards pushing monetary theory back to becoming a theory of output as a whole. But my lack of emancipation from preconceived ideas showed itself in what now seems to me to be the outstanding fault of the theoretical parts of that work (namely, Books III and IV), that I failed to deal thoroughly with the effects of *changes* in the level of output. My so-called "fundamental equations" were an instantaneous picture taken on the assumption of a given output. They attempted to show how, assuming the given output, forces could develop which involved a profit-disequilibrium, and thus required a change in the level of output. But the dynamic development, as distinct from the instantaneous picture, was left incomplete and extremely confused. This book, on the other hand, has evolved into what is primarily a study of the forces which determine changes in the scale of output and employment as a whole; and, whilst it is found that money enters into the economic scheme in an essential and peculiar manner, technical monetary detail falls into the background [*GT* p. xxii; italics in original].

Now, an author is not necessarily the best authority on the history of the development of his own work; and by definition he certainly is not an *objective* authority. This is particularly so when in the course of this development there takes place a radical change in the author's approach. In such circumstances we probably all have the understandable tendency to believe that the change occurred in our thinking earlier than it actually did—and Keynes was no exception. Thus I believe that in the foregoing passage he exaggerates the extent to

64

which he had "made progress" in the *Treatise* toward reinstating monetary theory as a "theory of output as a whole." And Keynes is certainly yielding to the temptation to rewrite the *Treatise* when later on in the *General Theory* (pp. 77–78) he states that in the *Treatise* he had argued "that change in the excess of investment over saving was the motive force governing changes in the volume of output"—and does not even mention changes in the price level![1]

But though we may have doubts about the accuracy of Keynes' timing of the change, I think that there can be little doubt that he correctly identified the nature of the change with his increased emphasis on analyzing variations in output. Indeed, as noted above (p. 54), the absence of an adequate analysis of such variations in the *Treatise* was actually pointed out to Keynes by Hawtrey a few months before its final publication, though Keynes did not reply until afterwards. Similarly, one of the criticisms of the "Cambridge Circus" in early 1931 revolved about the implicit assumption of constant output in Keynes' paradox of the widow's cruse—a criticism that Joan Robinson later published in her "Parable on Savings and Investment" (February 1933). On the other hand, as can be inferred from the description of the *Treatise* in Chapter 4 above, Keynes was certainly right when, in his letter of April 1932 to Joan Robinson on this article, he wrote:

> I think you are a little hard on me as regards the assumption of constant output. It is quite true that I have not followed out the consequences of changes of output in the earlier theoretical part. I admit that this wants doing, and I shall be doing it in my lectures; though that does not absolve me from being criticised for not having done it in my *Treatise*. But in my *Treatise* itself, I have long discussions with [?of] the effects of changes in output; it is only at a particular point in the preliminary theoretical argument that I assume constant output, and I am at pains to make this absolutely clear [*JMK* XIII, p. 270; brackets in source].

But in his answers to both Hawtrey and Joan Robinson, Keynes refers only to changes in output as such. He does not refer to what seems to me to be the really distinguishing mark of the *General Theory*, namely, the crucial role of changes in output as an *equilibrating force* with respect to aggregate demand and supply—or, equivalently, with respect to saving and investment. And this, of course, is

1. This passage appears already in the mid-1934 draft of the *General Theory* (*JMK* XIII, p. 437) and in the subsequent galley proofs (*JMK* XIV, pp. 426–27).

what lends crucial significance to Keynes' "fundamental psychological law" of a marginal propensity to consume which is less than unity: for (as Keynes repeatedly emphasizes) if it were unity, changes in output would have exactly the same effect on both aggregate demand and supply and so could not act as an equilibrating force.

On other occasions, however, Keynes did emphasize this distinguishing mark. Thus in a letter (dated 30 August 1936) that he wrote to Roy Harrod shortly after the appearance of the *General Theory*, in criticism of a draft of the latter's 1937 review article, Keynes said:

You don't mention *effective demand* or, more precisely, the demand schedule for output as a whole, except in so far as it is implicit in the multiplier. To me, the most extraordinary thing regarded historically, is the complete disappearance of the theory of the demand and supply for output as a whole, i.e. the theory of employment, *after* it had been for a quarter of a century the most discussed thing in economics.[2] One of the most important transitions for me, after my *Treatise on Money* had been published, was suddenly realising this. It only came after I had enunciated to myself the psychological law that, when income increases, the gap between income and consumption will increase,—a conclusion of vast importance to my own thinking but not apparently, expressed just like this, to anyone else's. Then, appreciably later, came the notion of interest as being the meaning of liquidity preference, which became quite clear in my mind the moment I thought of it. And last of all,[3] after an immense lot of muddling and many drafts, the proper definition of the marginal efficiency of capital linked up one thing with another [*JMK* XIV, p. 85; italics in original].

Similarly, in the reply he published in 1937 to Bertil Ohlin, Keynes wrote:

The novelty in my treatment of saving and investment consists, not in my maintaining their necessary aggregate equality, but in the proposition that it is, not the rate of interest, but the level of incomes which (in conjunction with certain other factors) ensures

2. Presumably, the quarter-century between the beginning of the Ricardo-Malthus debate on the possibility of a "general glut in the market" in 1820 and the appearance of J. S. Mill's *Principles of Political Economy* in 1848. See also the reference to this period in the *General Theory* (pp. 32–34).

3. I have at this point followed the text of the excerpt from this letter as it has been reproduced in the "Editorial Foreword" to the *General Theory* (p. xv); in *JMK* XIV, these words are incorrectly rendered as "last fall."

this equality. . . . The arguments which lead up to this initial conclusion are independent of my subsequent theory of the rate of interest, and in fact I reached it before I had reached the latter theory [*JMK* XIV, pp. 211–12].

In order to bring out the full flavor of this difference between the *General Theory* and the *Treatise*, consider the analysis in the latter of the impact of the sudden initiation of a "thrift campaign" on an economy which is originally in a savings-investment equilibrium. This campaign, says Keynes of the *Treatise*, will increase savings, thus generate losses, and thus

cause entrepreneurs to seek to protect themselves by throwing their employees out of work or reducing their wages. But even this will not improve their position, since the spending power of the public will be reduced by just as much as the aggregate costs of production. By however much entrepreneurs reduce wages and however many of their employees they throw out of work, they will continue to make losses so long as the community continues to save in excess of new investment. Thus there will be no position of equilibrium until either (a) all production ceases and the entire population starves to death; or (b) the thrift campaign is called off or peters out as a result of the growing poverty; or (c) investment is stimulated by some means or another so that its cost no longer lags behind the rate of saving [*TM* I, pp. 159–60].

This passage must be read against the background of the first fundamental equation, reproduced from Chapter 4 above:

$$(i)' \qquad P = \frac{E}{O} + \frac{I' - S}{R},$$

which is implicitly referred to in it. And what the passage says is that the reduction generated by growing unemployment and/or wage reductions in the "aggregate costs of production" (i.e., in E, the income of the *Treatise*) will cause "the spending power of the public"—and hence their consumption expenditures—to "be reduced just as much," so that the level of savings S remains unchanged, and still in excess of the cost of investment I'.[4]

In brief, it seems to me that Keynes is implicitly assuming here that the marginal propensity to spend is unity, so that a decline in

4. Keynes employed a similar argument in his unpublished "Notes on the Definition of Saving" which he prepared in March 1932 in connection with his discussion of Robertson's criticism of the *Treatise* (*JMK* XIII, pp. 276–78, 281).

output cannot reduce the excess of saving over investment and thus cannot act as an equilibrating force. Instead, the decline in output will come to an end only as the result of some chance exogenous force that closes the gap between saving and investment: "the thrift campaign is called off," or "investment is stimulated by some means or another." And the very way in which Keynes also refers to the vague possibility that equilibrium might also be reestablished if "the thrift campaign . . . peters out as a result of the growing poverty," reveals how far he was then from seeing how changes in output—and hence income—act as a systematic influence on saving, and hence (via a marginal propensity to consume which is less than unity) as a systematic equilibrating mechanism.

When did Keynes first begin to see this equilibrating mechanism? In his June 1931 Harris Foundation lecture, Keynes enthusiastically and unreservedly restated the theory of unemployment that he had just published in the *Treatise*. In the course of so doing, he explained how an excess of savings generates a decline in output, and then went on to say:

> Now there is a reason for expecting an equilibrium point of decline to be reached. A given deficiency of investment causes a given decline of profit. A given decline of profit causes a given decline of output. Unless there is a constantly increasing deficiency of investment, there is eventually reached, therefore, a sufficiently low level of output which represents a kind of spurious equilibrium [*JMK* XIII, pp. 355–56].

At first sight, this would seem to be an adumbration of the unemployment-equilibrium notion of the *General Theory*. But closer examination of the context in which this paragraph appears indicates that this is not the case. For this context is one in which Keynes is analyzing the forces which generate, not a continuing state of unemployment equilibrium, but the transitory stationary point at the trough of the business cycle. That is, what Keynes is analyzing here is the causes of the eventual elimination of the excess of saving over investment which generates the slump, and its replacement at the turning point of the cycle by an opposite excess which then begins to generate the recovery.

What further distinguishes this discussion sharply from that of the *General Theory* is the fact that Keynes' primary explanation of why the economy reaches the aforementioned turning point is not in terms of variations in saving (which "either varies in the wrong direction . . . or is substantially unchanged, or if it varies in the right direction, so as partly to compensate changes in investment, varies insufficiently," *JMK* XIII, p. 354), but in terms of variations in investment. In particular, "as soon as output begins to recover" (and Keynes does not really explain why this recovery occurs) "the tide is turned and the decline in fixed investment is partly offset by increased investment in working capital" (ibid., p. 355). All this is far removed from the noncyclical analysis of the *General Theory* of the way in which an initial decline in investment generates a decrease in output which continues until the systematic downward influence such a decrease exerts on saving brings the economy to a new equilibrium position in which saving is once again equal to investment at the new, lower level of the latter—a level which remains unchanged throughout the adjustment process.

Some indications of the aforementioned equilibrating mechanism are, however, to be found in a letter which Keynes wrote to Kahn in September 1931 and which unmistakably describes the equilibrating effect of changes in output (*JMK* XIII, pp. 373–75). Here Keynes effectively distinguishes (though without using the term) between the case in which the marginal propensity to spend is unity (so that an exogenous increase in output does not affect the discrepancy between saving and investment, and hence the level of profits: here, accordingly, such an exogenous increase will drive output to its "maximum") and the case in which "each level of aggregate output has an appropriate proportion of saving to incomes attached to it, e.g., if $S/E = f(O)$ or better . . .

$$\frac{S}{E} = f_1\left(\frac{E}{P}\right) + f_2\left(\frac{Q}{P}\right) \quad [E + Q = OP]"[5]$$

(so that changes in the level of output can act to close the gap between savings and investment and thus bring the economy to a position of zero profits "before O reaches maximum"; this is accordingly a position of " 'long-period unemployment,' i.e., an equilibrium position short of full employment"). I might note that this letter provides the first instance recorded in *JMK* XIII of Keynes' explicit use of a savings function.

There is a possibility that this letter may be related to a discussion which had appeared a few months before in Kahn's famous multiplier article. In particular, at one point in this article, Kahn (1931, pp. 8–10) digresses in order to address himself to the question of the relation of

---

5. Brackets in letter as published in *JMK* XIII. Keynes' notation here is that of the *Treatise*; see above, p. 34.

his argument to the fundamental equations of the *Treatise*. He then applies these equations, not (in *Treatise*-like fashion) to show how the excess of cost-of-investment over savings increases the price level of consumption goods, but to do just the opposite: namely, to show how—under conditions of unemployment, and hence of a perfectly elastic supply of consumption goods, whose price accordingly remains constant—an expansion of government investment ("however great may be the cost of the investment") will generate "secondary employment" to just that extent necessary to increase savings so as to keep "the difference between total savings and total investment at a constant amount (or, more accurately, at an amount that varies in direct proportion with the output of consumption-goods)" (ibid., p. 10, penultimate paragraph of Section IX). That is (in terms of the first fundamental equation, to which Kahn is clearly referring here), S will increase together with R to the extent necessary to keep $(I' - S)/R$ constant.

In this discussion we can discern the germ of the notion of a change in employment (and hence output) acting as a force to bring saving into some specified relation with investment. But in contrast with Keynes in his letter, Kahn does not in this context refer explicitly to the notion of equilibrium.[6] Indeed his sole purpose is to show that the fact "that under certain circumstances employment can be increased without any significant alteration in the difference between savings and investment—does not in the slightest degree invalidate the causal force of Mr. Keynes' argument [i.e., his fundamental equations]" (Kahn 1931, p. 10).

We should also remember that Kahn's discussion here is a digression from his major purpose in the article, which is to analyze and provide an estimate of the multiplier. Furthermore, the multiplier of Kahn's article is the dynamic one, showing in terms of a declining geometric series the sequence of "secondary employments" generated by a once-and-for-all increase in investment. It is not the comparative-statics multiplier, comparing an initial equilibrium position with the one generated by a permanently increased level of investment. And it should be emphasized that it is only the comparative-statics multiplier that is explicitly related to the notion of unemployment equilibrium which concerned Keynes in his letter of September 1931 and, of course, in his subsequent theory of effective demand.

It may also be of relevance in this context to note that the novelty

6. Kahn uses the term "equilibrium" only once in his article (1931, p. 12, n.1), and in a different context.

of Kahn's article did not lie in its pointing out that an increase in government investment would also generate "secondary employment." For months before Kahn had even begun to work on his article, Keynes had made this point in his May 1929 *Can Lloyd George Do It?* (*JMK* IX, pp. 104–7)—and even then it was probably not a new point. But the question which at that time could not be answered "with any sort of precision" (ibid. p. 107) was the extent of this "secondary employment." In particular, the puzzle was why the process did not continue indefinitely, i.e. why the additional spending generated by employing one additional worker would not lead to a sequence of additional spending by the other workers which would continue until the last of the unemployed had found work. The answer to this question was given by Kahn's analysis of leakages. Thus the major analytical contribution of Kahn's multiplier article was in its rigorous demonstration, not that the multiplier was greater than unity, but that it was less than infinity. I shall return to this point in Chapter 12 below (see especially n.15).

Let me sum up the discussion by saying that though Kahn's article clearly constituted a major step toward the *General Theory*, and though in retrospect we see that the theory of the multiplier can be formulated in a way which is logically equivalent to the theory of effective demand, I doubt very much if this equivalence was seen by the actors of our drama in 1931. And my doubts on this score are reinforced by the simple fact that—as we shall see from the account which follows—more than another year was to pass before Keynes finally formulated his theory of effective demand.

To continue with our account, the ideas which Keynes sketched out in his letter of September 1931 were developed by him more systematically (though this time without explicit use of the saving function) in the earliest surviving fragments—dating from the period 1931–32—of what was to become the *General Theory* (*JMK* XIII, pp. 381–89).[7] Here Keynes retains the definitions of the *Treatise*, but says that instead of defining changes in profits, ΔQ, as $\Delta I - \Delta S$ (as he does in the *Treatise*) he will adopt the "clearer . . . mode of expression," $\Delta Q = \Delta D - \Delta E$, where D represents total disbursement on consumption and investment goods, and E (as in the *Treatise*) is the

---

7. Unfortunately, Moggridge does not explain the nature of the evidence on which this dating is based. Thus the additional fragments that he describes as being from the "slightly later work, although still before the end of 1932" (*JMK* XIII, p. 380) and reproduces in *JMK* XIII, pp. 397–405 would actually seem to me to be the earlier ones: they are less finished than the ones on pp. 381–96 and, more important, they seem to be more closely related to the *Treatise* with its emphasis on the determination of the respective prices of consumption and investment goods.

total cost of production. Then Keynes proceeds once again to show how—under the assumption that "[consumption] spending decreases less than earnings decrease with investment stable"—changes in output can bring the economy to a position of zero profits at a level of output below that of full employment (*JMK* XIII, p. 387).

In this draft we can find the well-developed beginnings of many other major themes of the *General Theory*: the paradox of savings (*JMK* XIII, pp. 387–88);[8] the distinction between the effect of a wage reduction on an individual firm and on the economy as a whole (*JMK* XIII, pp. 390–94); and the fact that the " 'automatic' forces" generated by such an overall wage and price reduction act by increasing "the proportion of the stock of money to income," thereby creating a "growing relative abundance of money [which] will, unless the general desire for liquidity relatively to income is capable of increasing without limit, lead in due course to a decline in the rate of interest" which "exercis[es] a favourable influence on investment" (*JMK* XIII, pp. 395–96).

And in another fragment (still before the end of 1932)[9] we also find a reference to "the state of liquidity-preference (A) which tells us what ρ, the rate of interest exclusive of risk-allowance, will be, given to [the ?] quantity of money so that $\rho = A(M)$" (*JMK* XIII, pp. 397–98; square brackets in source). Similarly, this fragment contains a reference to the "marginal productivity of capital" (*JMK* XIII, p. 398), though the precise notion of the marginal rate of return on capital is still absent. Keynes also states that by determining the rate of interest by liquidity preference he can without circularity use this rate to value productive assets by means of discounting their expected quasi-rents (*JMK* XIII, pp. 398–400).

The voice is that of the *General Theory*: but the analytical framework is still largely that of the *Treatise*. For though there is no explicit reference in these surviving fragments to the fundamental equations themselves, the analysis, as we have seen, revolves about the effect of changes in output on the critical second term of these equations, namely, profits, $Q = I - S$, where all terms are defined as in the *Treatise*. Furthermore, this analysis does not yet contain any reference either to the aggregate demand function or to its component consumption and investment functions. It is also noteworthy that these functions are not mentioned in Joan Robinson's article "The Theory of Money and the Analysis of Output" that she published in

8. Cf. also the echoes of this theme in an unpublished note entitled "Historical Retrospect" which Keynes wrote in 1932 (*JMK* XIII, p. 407).
9. See n.7 above.

the first issue of the *Review of Economic Studies* in October 1933—an article that (in her words, eighteen years later) "gives an outline of Keynes' theory as far as it had got in 1933" (Joan Robinson 1951, p. viii).[10] Nor do such functions appear in the notes which R. B. Bryce took of Keynes' lectures at Cambridge during October–November 1932. As might be expected, these notes show many other similarities with the mid-1932 draft.[11]

All this is changed by mid-1934 at the latest, by which time Keynes had written draft chapters (reproduced in *JMK* XIII, pp. 424–56) whose terminology and basic analytical structure are already those of the *General Theory of Employment, Interest, and Money*—which full title is now used for the first time.[12] In particular this draft distinguishes between the "actual and anticipated" values of the various macroeconomic magnitudes (a distinction to which, Keynes says, "insufficient attention" was given in the *Treatise*) and accordingly explicitly abandons the definitions of the *Treatise* which permitted actual savings and investment to differ (*JMK* XIII, pp. 434–37; see also *JMK* XIV, p. 179).

As he was frequently to do in the final form of the *General Theory*,[13] Keynes now measures his macroeconomic magnitudes in

10. More recently, Mrs. Robinson has described this article as an "interim report" which "clears the ground for the new theory but does not supply it" (1966, p. viii). It would be very surprising if this article had not—like Joan Robinson's earlier *Economica* article—been discussed with Keynes. There is, however, no reference to it in *JMK* XIII, though this absence may well be due to the already noted fact that very few records survive of the discussions that Keynes carried out during 1933.

11. Robert B. Bryce (1910–) was a Canadian who had come to Cambridge in the fall of 1932 to study economics after completing his B.A. at the University of Toronto. During the three successive academic years 1932–33, 1933–34, and 1934–35, he took fairly detailed notes of Keynes' lectures on monetary economics (see the beginning of this chapter). These notes were first cited by Moggridge (1973, p. 82; *JMK* XIII, pp. 343 and 411). A recently typed version of the handwritten originals (which are still in the possession of Mr. Bryce) is filed in the Keynes' Papers. Of Bryce's subsequent role in bringing the word of Keynes to Harvard and then to Canada, see Galbraith (1965), p. 137. I am greatly indebted to Robert Bryce (now and for many years a senior Canadian government official), Lord Kahn, and Donald Moggridge for providing me with a photocopy of the typed notes and permitting me to refer to them here.

Further evidence that Keynes formulated his theory of effective demand after 1932 is provided by a comment in Keynes' 1937 lectures at Cambridge which would seem to indicate that he "reached the conception of effective demand" after 1931–32 (*JMK* XIV, p. 180).

12. The title of the table of contents from Dec. 1933 was "The General Theory of Employment" (*JMK* XIII, p. 421). There is no indication in *JMK* XIII of the title that Keynes had in mind when he wrote the draft chapters from 1931–32 already discussed. However, Moggridge tells us that the title of Keynes' lectures in the autumn of 1932 was "The Monetary Theory of Production" and remained unchanged the following autumn (*JMK* XIII, pp. 343, 420). This was also the title of Keynes' 1933 contribution to the Spiethoff festschrift which Keynes concluded with a reference to "the task on which I am now occupying myself" (*JMK* XIII, p. 411).

13. Though, interestingly enough, not in Chap. 3, "The Principle of Effective De-

terms of "wage units," by which he means their real purchasing
power in terms of units of labor, i.e., their respective money values
divided by the money wage rate W (*JMK* XIII, p. 441). Such real
variables are denoted by the subscript w. Keynes then proceeds to
develop his theory of effective demand—which in this draft sometimes means a schedule, but more frequently means the demand for
total output that actually becomes effective in the economy (*JMK*
XIII, p. 439). First he defines the "employment function"

$$D_w = F(N),$$

"where an effective demand equal to D_w leads to N units of labour
being employed" (*JMK* XIII, p. 440). In the final terminology of the
General Theory (see our next chapter), this is the "aggregate supply
function"—a term which is conspicuously absent from the 1934
draft.[14] In present-day terminology, this is clearly the production
function—relating the output of goods to the input of labor, which in
this context represents all variable factors of production.

Keynes goes on to provide fairly detailed descriptions of the
"propensity to consume [which] may be expressed by the functional
relationship

$$C_w = f_1(N, r, E)$$

which means that C_w will be the amount of consumption measured in
wage units when real income is what results from an amount of employment N, and when r is the rate of interest and E the state of
long-term expectations." Similarly, "the propensity to invest is expressed by the functional relationship

$$I_w = f_2(N, r, E)."$$

---

mand," which corresponds most closely to this portion of the 1934 draft. For further
details, see the next chapter.

14. And which continues to be conspicuously absent from all three galley proofs. In
these proofs (which were run off during the first half of 1935) Keynes continues to use
the term "employment function," though he now writes it as $D' = f(N)$ and describes
D' as "the supply price" (*JMK* XIV, p. 370). In the third proof, D' is also described as
"the aggregate·cost of production" (*JMK* XIV, p. 374). Thus the actual term "supply
function" appears for the first time only in the published form of the *General Theory*,
where it is denoted as $Z = \phi(N)$. These points will be further discussed in the next
chapter. It seems likely that one of the reasons that led Keynes to abandon the D'
notation was its misleading nature. Thus in a note which Robertson added in 1949 on
his 1935 correspondence with Keynes on this point, he wrote: " 'But fancy labelling a
supply curve D'?' " (*JMK* XIII, p. 520, n.17; see also Robertson 1955, p. 474). I might
also note that the "employment function" of the published *General Theory* is the
inverse of the one presented in the 1934 draft and in the galley proofs. Thus, for example, the employment function (for the r-th industry) in the published book is denoted as $N_r = F_r(D_w)$ (*GT* p. 280).

However, says Keynes, "we shall argue in what follows that, given the propensities to spend and to invest, consumption will depend mainly on N and investment mainly on r and E. Thus the simplified expressions

$$C_w = f_1(N) \quad \text{and} \quad I_w = f_2(r, E)$$

may sometimes be legitimate" (*JMK* XIII, p. 441). It is noteworthy that Keynes here already defines "the marginal yield (or efficiency) of capital" which determines the point to which investment "will be pushed" when we have "from some other source ascertain[ed] the rate of interest" (*JMK* XIII, pp. 452–53). From all this it then follows that "the level of employment, given the propensities to spend and to invest, is given by the value of N which satisfies the equation

$$F(N) = f_1(N, r, E) + f_2(N, r, E)"$$

(*JMK* XIII, p. 442).

Because of Keynes' failure to formulate this argument in terms of a demand-and-supply mechanism, the explanation of the determination of the equilibrium level of employment is indeed more mechanical than the explanation (albeit inadequate) in terms of dynamic market forces in the final form of the *General Theory* (see p. 92 below). At the same time it is worth noting that the exposition of this mid-1934 draft is more systematic and mathematically elegant than the one which finally appeared in the *General Theory*. Thus, as we have seen, the 1934 draft provides mathematical descriptions of both the consumption and investment functions (whereas an explicit description of the latter is curiously absent from the *General Theory*!) and explicitly introduces expectations as one of their variables. It also follows the more elegant procedure of first describing these functions in a symmetric, general form[15] and then proceeding to specify the additional assumptions by which this general form is reduced to the different specific forms in which the consumption and investment functions are actually employed in the analysis. Finally it explains the determination of the equilibrium level of unemployment as the solution of an explicitly presented equation.

Now, it is true that all of these points are fully expounded in a

---

15. Cf. Hicks's later advocacy of this symmetry in his famous "Mr. Keynes and the 'Classics' " (1937), p. 47. In his subsequent letter to Hicks on this article, Keynes explained that he had dropped the original symmetric form of his investment function because "it overemphasizes current income. In the case of the inducement to invest, expected income for the period of the investment is the relevant variable" (*JMK* XIV, p. 80).

literary fashion in the *General Theory* as published. Nevertheless, it is worth noting that—to judge from the subsequent rapid acceptance of the Hicks-Modigliani *IS-LM* model as the standard interpretation of the *General Theory*—the revealed preference of the profession is actually for the more formal style of presentation of the analysis that Keynes used in his 1934 draft, as against his presentation in the final form of the *General Theory*.

There are two further points about the mid-1934 draft that I would like to mention. First of all, though in the passages cited above there is (as just noted) no explanation of the equilibrium position in terms of the demand-and-supply mechanism, an attempted explanation in terms of profit maximization is given at an earlier point in the draft. At this point Keynes presents the following, somewhat obscure, argument:

> The *quasi-rent* (Q) from a given output of finished goods we have already defined in chapter 4 as being the excess of the expected sale proceeds of the goods over their prime cost (NW). Thus the sum of the quasi-rent and prime cost of a given output is equal to the effective demand for it, i.e. $D = Q + NW$, which may also be written $D_w = Q_w + N$.
>
> Now, a firm's capital equipment being given, there is, each day, the question of the train of employment to be set going that day which will maximize the firm's quasi-rent. Under normal assumptions of competition etc. the condition of maximum quasi-rent will be satisfied by a volume of employment such that the prime cost of the marginal employment will be equal to the expected sale proceeds of the resulting increment of product. For the sake of simplicity and clearness of exposition, we shall, therefore, assume in what follows that we are dealing with this case . . . . We shall assume, that is to say, that employment will be carried to a point at which $\Delta D_w = \Delta N$, and that $(d\,D_w)/(d\,N)$ is the real wage. . . .
>
> Now so long as ΔD_w is greater than ΔN it will pay the entrepreneurs to increase their demand for employment; and so long as $(d\,D_w)/(d\,N)$ is greater than the marginal disutility it will pay workers to increase their offer of employment. Thus the volume of employment can come to equilibrium either because ΔD_w would be less than ΔN if employment were to be further increased, or because no more labour is forthcoming at a real wage not greater than $(d\,D_w)/(d\,N)$. The reader will remember that according to the classical theory, $\Delta D_w = \Delta N$ for *all* values of N, so that the volume of employment always comes to equilibrium at

the point at which $(d\,D_w)/(d\,N)$ is equal to the marginal disutility of labour. We, however, are envisaging the possibility that in general ΔD_w is *not* equal to ΔN, so that a limit may be set to a further increase of employment by the fact that for the values of N in excess of a certain figure ΔD_w would be *less* than ΔN [*JMK* XIII, pp. 425–27; italics in original].

Thus Keynes' analysis implies that the position of unemployment equilibrium is determined by the condition $(\Delta D_w)/(\Delta N) = 1$. This conclusion, however, is inconsistent with the analysis which Keynes presents at other points in this draft. For if D_w in this passage denotes the same thing as the $D_w = F(N)$ of the employment function in the passage cited on p. 74 above, then—as Keynes points out later in this draft (*JMK* XIII, p. 446)—the slope of this curve is unitary throughout.[16] Hence the condition $(\Delta D_w)/\Delta N$ cannot serve to determine a unique position of unemployment equilibrium.

On the other hand, if despite the fact that Keynes of the 1934 draft does *not* explicitly define D_w as the sum of the consumption and investment functions (i.e., as what he was later to denote as the aggregate demand function), we choose nevertheless to interpret it that way,[17] then Keynes' assumption that the marginal propensity to consume is less than unity (which he makes at a later point in this draft)[18] implies that there does not exist any point which satsfies the condition $(\Delta D_w)/\Delta N = 1$![19]

Whether because of these inconsistencies, or because of other reasons, the fact remains that Keynes omitted from the subsequent drafts of the *General Theory* the reference to $(\Delta D_w)/\Delta N = 1$ as the

16. Keynes states that this will be the case only under certain assumptions with respect to the distribution of income. This proviso, however, does not affect my present argument. See also Keynes' proof in the published form of the *General Theory* (p. 55, n.2) that the aggregate supply function (which corresponds to the employment function here; see n.14 above) has a unitary slope throughout. This is further discussed in the next chapter; see p. 87.

17. And there is some ambiguity on this point. For Keynes' statement in the last paragraph of the passage just cited that "according to the classical theory, $\Delta D_w = \Delta N$ for all values of N" makes sense only if he is indeed regarding D_w as the sum of these functions; cf. the corresponding passages in the published form of the *General Theory* (pp. 25–26 and 29), which are also discussed in the next chapter, pp. 85 and 89.

18. See *JMK* XIII, p. 445. I am here also making use of Keynes' assumption that the investment function does not depend on N.

19. Though it is meaningless in the present context, I might note that a point at which $(\Delta D_w/\Delta N) = 1$ would be one at which the aggregate demand curve is parallel to the 45° aggregate supply curve, so that (on the assumption of concavity) the distance between them is a maximum. If, on the other hand, we take account of the assumption that the marginal propensity to spend is less than unity and is declining, then this distance is at a maximum at the origin, i.e., where $N = O$!

profit-maximizing condition which determines the position of unemployment equilibrium.[20] I shall return in the next chapter to the significance of this fact for an understanding of the published form of
the *General Theory* (p. 93 below).

My second point about the 1934 draft also relates to profit-
maximization. I have contended above that Keynes was so interested
in presenting the *General Theory* as a further development of the
Treatise, that he yielded to the temptation to rewrite the *Treatise*
when he referred to it (above, p. 65). Let me now suggest that (as is
only natural) the earlier the draft of the *General Theory*, the more
prone Keynes was to succumb to this temptation. Thus in comparing
the *General Theory* with the *Treatise* in his mid-1934 draft, Keynes
writes:

> In my *Treatise on Money* the concept of changes in the excess of
> investment over saving as there defined was a way of handling
> changes in quasi-rent, or rather, since I did not in that book
> distinguish clearly between expected and realised results—in en-
> trepreneurs' profits. I there argued that change in the excess of
> investment over saving was the motive force governing change in
> the volume of output. Thus the new argument, though (as I now
> think) it was made more accurate and instructive, is no more than
> a development of the old.
>
> Expressed in the language of my *Treatise on Money*, it would
> run:—the expectation of an increased excess of investment over
> saving, given the former volume of employment and output, will
> induce entrepreneurs to increase the volume of employment and
> output. Both arguments depend on the discovery, if it can be
> called such, that an increase in the sum of consumption and
> investment will be associated with an increase in entrepreneurs'
> profit and that the expectation of an increase in entrepreneurs'
> profit will be associated with a higher level of employment and
> output. The significance of both lies in their attempt to show that
> the volume of employment is determined by the efforts of the
> entrepreneurs to maximise the excess of investment over saving
> as defined in my *Treatise on Money* [*JMK* XIII, pp. 436–37].

Now, as I have already noted, the misleading contention in the
first paragraph of this passage that in the *Treatise*, too, profits were
"the motive force governing changes in the volume of output" also

20. Thus compare the passage just cited from the 1934 draft with the roughly corresponding passages in the galley proofs (*JMK* XIV, pp. 425–26) and in the published
version (*GT* pp. 53–54), respectively.

appears in the corresponding passage of the final form of the *General Theory* (pp. 77–78). But what we do not find in this corresponding passage is the even more misleading implication at the end of the second paragraph just cited that the analysis of the *Treatise* too was based on the principle of profit maximization.[21] For, as I have already emphasized, Keynes of the *Treatise* considered the marginal analysis of value theory to be outside his terms of reference. So too, correspondingly, was the principle of profit maximization. Indeed, neither the term nor concept "profit maximization" appears in the *Treatise*. I shall return to this point, too, in the next chapter (pp. 92–93; see also above, pp. 13 and 47).

I have argued above that the theory of effective demand which Keynes presented in his mid-1934 draft was formulated by him after the fall of 1932. By making use again (see n.11 above) of Robert Bryce's lecture notes, we can, however, further narrow the possible time period. In particular, these notes show that the lectures which Keynes gave in October-November 1933 were very similar to his presentation in the mid-1934 draft.[22] We can therefore conclude that Keynes formulated his theory of effective demand during 1933, and in all probability during the first half of that year.[23]

21. Note that this implication had already been deleted from the corresponding passages in the galley proofs (*JMK* XIV, p. 427).

22. Thus Bryce's notes on Keynes' lecture of 4 December 1933 read as follows:
We have
$$Y = C + I$$
In a given state of the news [denoted by w] C is a function of Y. $[C] = \phi_1(w, Y)$.
I is a function of the state of the news [and the rate of interest, denoted by ρ] $= \phi_2(w, \rho)$
i.e. $Y = \phi_1(Y) + \phi_2(\rho)$ when w given.
Hence it is largely ρ that is important.
Suppose N total number of men employed
N_1 producing for consumption
N_2 producing for investment
$N = N_1 + N_2$
Then $N_1 = f_1(N)$ $N_2 = f_2(\rho)$ (r. of i.)
$N = f_1(N) + f_2(\rho)$.

Matter in square brackets is mine. The parallelism with the excerpt from the mid-1934 draft cited above is unmistakable. (There seem to be inaccuracies in this passage in the form in which it appears in the typed version of these notes that is filed in the Keynes Papers. Accordingly, I have here amended the text of that version on the basis of a photocopy of the original handwritten notes with which Robert Bryce has kindly provided me).

23. See Moggridge (1973), pp. 81–83. Keynes' *Means to Prosperity*, which he wrote in March 1933, does not help us fix the date any more precisely; for this pamphlet is essentially a popular application to the specific problems of Britain of Richard Kahn's 1931 multiplier article, and does not specify the broader theoretical framework that underlies its policy proposals. (For further details on this pamphlet, see Chapter 12 below, nn.6, 8, and 11 and the text there.) That by the end of 1933 Keynes had already

Let me now return to that most revealing letter to Roy Harrod cited above on page 66. As will be recalled, in addition to the theory of effective demand, this letter lists two other notions that Keynes considered among the major contributions of the *General Theory*: liquidity preference and the marginal efficiency of capital. In contrast to the theory of effective demand, however, neither of these notions is an innovation of the *General Theory* itself. In the case of the theory of liquidity preference, Keynes was indeed the innovator: but he had already made the essence of the innovation in the *Treatise*. And in the case of the marginal efficiency of capital, Keynes himself pointed out in the *General Theory* that this concept is identical to Irving Fisher's concept of "the rate of return over cost" in his *Theory of Interest* (1930, pp. 155–61).[24] In Keynes' words, "Professor Fisher uses his 'rate of return over cost' in the same sense and precisely for the same purpose as I employ the 'marginal efficiency of capital' " (*GT* p. 141).

I should, however, note that to all appearances, Keynes arrived at this concept independently of Fisher.[25] In any event, when Keynes first used this concept in his mid-1934 draft of the *General Theory* he did not refer to Fisher (*JMK* XIII, p. 453). Nor does the paragraph in the *General Theory* in which Keynes acknowledges Fisher's prior development of this concept appear in the first and second proofs of the book, which were circulated for criticism in early 1935 (*JMK* XIV, pp. 351, 463).[26] The first record in *JMK* XIII of Keynes' recognition of Fisher's priority—albeit, a much more qualified recognition than that which (to Keynes' credit) finally appeared in the *General*

---

formulated his theory of effective demand is also indicated by the fact that his table of contents from December 1933 refers for the first time to "Book III: Employment as a Function of the Motives to Spend and Invest" (*JMK* XIII, p. 421).

24. Actually, Fisher had already developed this concept in his *Rate of Interest* (1907), of which the *Theory of Interest* is in part a revision. In the former work, the concept is denoted as "the rate of return on sacrifice" (Fisher 1907, pp. 152–56).

25. This is also the view of Schumpeter (1954, p. 1178, n.15), who goes on to "testify to the fact" that Keynes "inserted the acknowledgment in question upon his attention's [sic] having been drawn to Fisher's formulation." The identity of the person who allegedly did so is, however, not indicated by Schumpeter. In an essay on Irving Fisher a few years ago, Samuelson (1967, p. 32, n.11) "seem[ed] to recall it was Redvers Opie." In this context it is of significance that Opie was at Oxford in the early 1930's and during this time was also in contact with Schumpeter, whose *Theory of Economic Development* (1934) he was then translating from the original German. See the "Translator's Note" to this book. (I am indebted to Paul Samuelson and Walter Salant for informative discussions of this point.)

26. This is the paragraph whose absence in the proofs of the *General Theory* reproduced at the top of p. 463 of *JMK* XIV is explicitly noted by the editor. The paragraph is, however, erroneously described as beginning on line 27 of p. 140 of the *General Theory*, instead of on line 24.

Theory—occurs in a letter which Keynes wrote to Roy Harrod in August 1935 (*JMK* XIII, p. 549).

I have already noted that the essence of the theory of liquidity preference appears in the *Treatise*. Needless to say, this theory is not developed in that book with the rigor and precision that characterize its development in the *General Theory*. Thus the latter has a more systematic discussion of the influence on the demand for money of uncertainty with respect to future interest rates.[27] Furthermore, the *Treatise* does not adequately explicate the systematic positive influence on the demand for money of an increase in income—and the systematic negative influence of an increase in interest. This failure is probably related to the already noted failure of the *Treatise* to present (as, of course, the *General Theory* does) an explicit demand function for money in terms of these variables (see the beginning of Chapter 6 above).

There is another significant difference between the liquidity-preference theory of the *General Theory* and its prototype in the *Treatise*. In particular, the securities of the *Treatise* are primarily equity securities; furthermore, Keynes does not distinguish between these securities and capital goods. Thus the portfolio-choice model of the *Treatise* is effectively a two-asset one: money and equity securities. In contrast, the corresponding model of the *General Theory* is effectively a two-stage three-asset model. Keynes (I think) still does not distinguish between capital goods and equity securities; but he now rarely uses the term "securities,"[28] and tends instead to speak specifically of "bonds" or "debts" as the alternative to holding money. In the first stage, then, the individual compares the marginal efficiency of capital with the going rate of interest in the market and on that basis chooses between holding physical capital (or equities)

---

27. The contrast between the respective roles of uncertainty in the *Treatise* and *General Theory* is even greater with respect to the theory of investment. To a certain extent, however, this may reflect, not an increased awareness of the importance of uncertainty per se, but the fact that Keynes of the *Treatise* considered the detailed analysis of investment to be outside his terms of reference (see page 47 above).

28. The only references to "securities" that I have been able to find in the *General Theory* are on pp. 94, 155, 197, and 200. Furthermore, from the context of the discussion on pp. 94 and 200—and from the fact that Keynes refers on both these occasions to "securities and other assets"—I get the impression that by "securities" Keynes now means bonds. This is clearly the case for the discussion on p. 197, where Keynes refers to open-market purchases of "very short-dated securities." I might also note that though the index to the *General Theory* lists discussions of "Securities, price of" as taking place on pp. 94, 199–200, 206, the term does not appear on p. 206, which instead refers to the "price of debts." Since, however, this index was not compiled by Keynes himself, but by D. M. Bensusan-Butt (*GT* p. xxiii), I do not know how significant this fact is.

and holding other liquid assets. Then on the basis of comparing the present rate of interest with his anticipation of the future rate, he chooses between holding these liquid assets in the form of long-term bonds or in the form of money (*GT* pp. 169–70, esp. p. 170, n.1, and pp. 173–74).

There are two further observations that I would like to make on this point. First, Keynes' dissatisfaction with the exposition of the *Treatise* began even before he developed his notion of the marginal efficiency of capital. Thus in his fall 1932 lectures at Cambridge (as Moggridge tells us) "Keynes distinguished liquidity preference from the state of bearishness of the *Treatise* by stating that the latter idea muddled up assets and debts against money while the former concentrated on debts and money alone" (*JMK* XIII, p. 412).[29]

Second, Keynes did not make a hard-and-fast distinction between the nature of the two stages delineated in the *General Theory*. In particular, in his subsequent article "The General Theory of Employment" (*Quarterly Journal of Economics*, 1937), he identified the first stage with the decision as to whether or not to hold money, and the second stage with the decision that has to be made by "the owner of wealth, who has been induced not to hold his wealth in the form of hoarded money" and who must then choose between holding his wealth in the form of bonds or "some kind of capital asset" (*JMK* XIV, p. 117). So I do not think that there is any significant misrepresentation of Keynes' views in saying that he conceived of the individual as deciding on his optimum portfolio by means of a simultaneous choice among all three alternative assets—money, bonds, and capital assets.

29. Note the clear echo of this statement on pp. 173–74 of the *General Theory*.

9. The theory of effective demand in the *General Theory*

In all probability, economists under the age of forty—and that means the majority of economists today—learned the theory of effective demand as just another chapter in their introductory course in economics. Indeed, the familiar diagonal-cross diagram that illustrates this theory may well have adorned the dustjacket of their textbook in this course. Accordingly, it may be difficult for them to conceive of the revolutionary impact that this theory had when Keynes first presented it. And it was revolutionary!

Testimony to this impact has been given by many elders of our profession who (in Samuelson's words) were "born as economists prior to 1936" (1946, p. 315). And though my "birthyear" was about a decade after this date, I began my studies before the theory of effective demand had percolated down to the introductory course in the field. So I, too, can still remember how strange and even difficult it was for me during my later graduate studies to have to learn to think in terms of a demand for aggregate output as a whole—a demand that was in some way conceptually different from actual aggregate income, as if national income expended could somehow differ from national income received!

Similarly, it had been thoroughly ingrained into us[1] that the demand function for a good could be defined only under the assumption of ceteris paribus. Indeed, in order to insure that this assumption was fulfilled in practice, the more punctilious economists of those days were only willing to speak of the demand function for an unimportant good (from the viewpoint of the total expenditure upon it), the variations of whose price would accordingly leave the "marginal utility of money" essentially constant. How then could one validly speak of a demand function for the aggregate of all goods taken together? How was it possible for "other things to be held constant" in such a case?

Because of the revolutionary impact of Keynes' theory of effective demand—as well as the fact that it is such a central feature of the *General Theory*, and so representative of both the strengths and weaknesses of Keynes' analytical style—I would like now to elabo-

---

1. And I am indebted to Abba Lerner for reminding me of this.

rate upon Keynes' presentation of it in its final form in his Chapter 3, "The Principle of Effective Demand." Another reason for this elaboration is that this chapter remains one of the most problematic in the *General Theory*: a fact that is well attested by Keynes' long and inconclusive discussions with Hawtrey on the proofs of this chapter during 1935 (*JMK* XIII, pp. 568, 597, 610, 623–24), and the even longer series of articles that have continued to appear over the years since its publication (particularly in the pages of the *Economic Journal*) in criticism of the concepts of this chapter, as well as in the attempt to explain what Keynes meant by it.[2] I might note that as a result of my now rereading this chapter against the background of the *Treatise*, I have understood certain points that were not clear to me in the past;[3] but as will be seen from what follows, some basic logical difficulties remain.

Before discussing Keynes' exposition of this theory, let me note that he saw it as the solution of "the great puzzle of effective demand" with which Malthus had unsuccessfully "wrestled" in his famous debate with Ricardo—which "puzzle" had then "vanished from economic literature. You will not find it mentioned even once in the whole works of Marshall, Edgeworth and Professor Pigou, from whose hands the classical theory has received its most mature embodiment. It could only live on furtively, below the surface, in the underworlds of Karl Marx, Silvio Gesell or Major Douglas" (*GT* p. 32). Surprisingly enough, Keynes did not include here in his list of "underworlds" the one associated with those "amateur American economists (cranks, some might say), Rorty and Johannsen," with whose theories of oversaving Keynes had expressed "strong sympathy" in the *Treatise* (II, pp. 89–90). What makes this omission even more surprising is that Johannsen's book *A Neglected Point In Connection with Crises* (1908), whose analysis Keynes had briefly summarized in the *Treatise* (II, p. 90, n.2), contained a discussion of what Johannsen (1908, pp. 43ff) called the "Multiplying Principle," which is similar in general conception (though definitely not in analytical precision) to Richard Kahn's multiplier!

2. See, e.g., Patinkin (1949), de Jong (1954, 1955), Hawtrey (1954, 1956), Robertson (1955), Weintraub (1957; 1958, chap. 2), Wells (1962), Davidson (1962; 1972, chap. 3), and Millar (1972). See also Dillard (1948, pp. 30ff), Hansen (1953, pp. 29ff), as well as the additional references at the end of Millar's article.

3. In this connection let me explicitly and belatedly concede to de Jong and Wells that the contention of my 1949 article that there is no supply curve in the *General Theory* was based on a complete and inexcusable failure at the time to understand Keynes' notion of aggregate supply price (see n.12 below). This chapter is my attempt to amend this error. In this attempt I shall make use, where appropriate, of the references cited in the preceding footnote. This, however, is not meant to imply that the authors cited there would necessarily accept the following interpretation.

Let me turn now to the details of Keynes' theory of effective demand. Keynes first states that he will

> call the aggregate income (i.e. factor cost *plus* profit) resulting from a given amount of employment the *proceeds* of that employment. On the other hand, the aggregate supply price of the output of a given amount of employment is the expectation of proceeds which will just make it worth the while of the entrepreneurs to give that employment [*GT* p. 24; italics in original].

And in a footnote to this passage Keynes explicitly states that he is "deducting the user cost both from the *proceeds* and from the *aggregate supply price* of a given volume of output" (italics in original). Let me also note that in this chapter Keynes uses the term "aggregate demand price" interchangeably with "proceeds" (*GT* pp. 26, 28).

We then come to the critical passage in which Keynes summarizes his theory in the following words:

> Let Z be the aggregate supply price of the output from employing N men, the relationship between Z and N being written $Z = \phi(N)$, which can be called the *aggregate supply function*. Similarly, let D be the proceeds which entrepreneurs expect to receive from the employment of N men, the relationship between D and N being written $D = f(N)$, which can be called the *aggregate demand function*.
>
> Now if for a given value of N the expected proceeds are greater than the aggregate supply price, i.e. if D is greater than Z, there will be an incentive to entrepreneurs to increase employment beyond N and, if necessary, to raise costs by competing with one another for the factors of production, up to the value of N for which Z has become equal to D. Thus the volume of employment is given by the point of intersection between the aggregate demand function and the aggregate supply function; for it is at this point that the entrepreneurs' expectation of profits will be maximised. The value of D at the point of the aggregate demand function, where it is intersected by the aggregate supply function, will be called *the effective demand* [*GT* p. 25; italics in original].

A few pages later, Keynes repeats this argument as follows:

> Thus, given the propensity to consume and the rate of new investment, there will be only one level of employment consistent with equilibrium; since any other level will lead to inequality

between the aggregate supply price of output as a whole and its aggregate demand price [*GT* p. 28].

I must note that the conditional clause in the first of the preceding passages—"and, if necessary, to raise costs by competing with one another for the factors of production"—does not really apply to Keynes' discussion that follows, in which, for simplicity, he temporarily assumes that factor costs remain constant. In Keynes' words:

> In this summary we shall assume that the money-wage and other factor costs are constant per unit of labour employed. But this simplification, with which we shall dispense later, is introduced solely to facilitate the exposition. The essential character of the argument is precisely the same whether or not money-wages, etc., are liable to change [*GT* p. 27].

At first glance, these passages are very reminiscent of the general approach of the *Treatise*. For, as Keynes himself emphasizes (*GT*, pp. 77–78), the focus of the analysis is once again on entrepreneurial profits, which act as the motive force of the economy. And once again these profits are described by the difference between a demand price and a supply price—albeit "aggregate prices," which, Keynes warns us, are "not to be confused . . . with the [say] supply price of a unit of output in the ordinary[4] sense of this term" (*GT* p. 24 n.). As I noted on p. 75 above, Keynes did not make explicit use of the demand-and-supply mechanism in his 1934 presentation of the theory of effective demand. Nor does such a mechanism appear in any other of Keynes' writings on the subject at that time (cf. *JMK* XIII, pp. 457–58, 477–84).[5] Correspondingly, I would conjecture that Keynes subsequently introduced this mechanism into the analysis—and in particular, the difference between demand price and supply price—in an attempt to provide a more adequate dynamic explanation of the forces that bring the economy to the equilibrium level of employment. At the same time, I must emphasize that this dynamic analysis received scant attention even in the final form of the *General Theory*: indeed, it is barely adverted to outside of Chapter 3. Furthermore, as

4. I.e., Marshallian. But in one instance at least Marshall, too, used the term "price" to mean "aggregate price": see *Principles* (8th ed.), p. 838, line 13, as discussed in Patinkin (1963), p. 86, n.2. See also n.14 below.

5. It does, however, already appear in Bryce's notes of Keynes' lecture of 29 October 1934. But there is no corresponding discussion in the notes for fall 1933—which is consistent with the fact that the mechanism is not mentioned in the mid-1934 draft.

I shall contend below, it was not a successful analysis, and, in part, this lack of success was due to the actually misleading nature of the attempted parallelisms with the *Treatise* that have just been noted.

Be that as it may, the reader of Chapter 3 of the *General Theory* can feel justifiably exasperated by Keynes' failure to illustrate it with a diagram displaying the properties of his intersecting demand and supply functions. How many painful struggles to understand this chapter could thereby have been avoided! And how much of the resulting protracted and involved exegetical debates about its meaning could also have been avoided! (If the reader detects a personal note in these remarks, he is right). But, as I have already observed, for some reason Keynes did not, with one exception, make use of analytical diagrams in any of his writings (above, p. 21).

What makes this failure particularly exasperating is that Chapter 3 together with a lengthy footnote[6] in Chapter 6 contain ingredients that Keynes could have readily combined into a helpful diagrammatic presentation of his argument. And this presentation could have been particularly simple if Keynes had defined his variables in terms of wage units, as he did indeed define them in the aforementioned footnote, though not in Chapter 3.

Fig. 9.1 is an attempt to render such a presentation. (For the moment the symbols in the square brackets in this diagram should be ignored.) D_w and Z_w in this diagram represent, respectively, aggregate demand and supply measured in wage units. The positive, less-than-unity slope of the aggregate demand function $f(N)$ is such a familiar part of the *General Theory* as to require no further explanation. Insofar as the aggregate supply curve, $\phi(N)$, is concerned, this represents Keynes' assumptions that (a) user cost is neglected and (b) "factor cost bears a constant ratio to wage cost," so that N represents all variable-factor inputs. It then follows that $\phi(0) = 0$ and "$\phi'(N) = 1$" (quoted from Keynes' aforementioned note).[7] For under the foregoing assumptions, the total variable costs corresponding to a

----

6. This footnote (*GT* p. 55, n.2) goes back to a discussion in the text of the mid-1934 draft (*JMK* XIII, p. 446), which seems to have been deleted from the subsequent proofs of the *General Theory* and reinserted only in the final version (cf. *JMK* XIV, pp. 398–418).

7. The argument of this note (which is admittedly not too clear) can be reformulated as follows. Under assumption (a) in the text here, the aggregate supply price equals total variable costs, or $Z = WN + QT$, where Q and T respectively represent the price and quantity of variable factors other than labor. Keynes' assumption (b) can then be expressed as $(WN + QT)/WN = k = $ const. It follows that $Z = (kW)N$, where kW represents the "price" of variable-factors-of-production-in-general, whose quantity is represented by N. Hence $Z_w = Z/kW = \phi(N) \equiv N$, so that $\phi'(N) \equiv 1$. I understand the term "proceeds of the marginal product" in Keynes' note to refer to the additional proceeds that entrepreneurs insist upon in order to make it just worth their while to

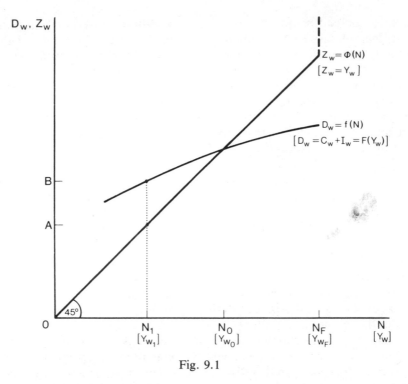

Fig. 9.1

given level of employment, hence the "proceeds" (net of user cost) "which will just make it worth the while of entrepreneurs to give that employment," and hence the "aggregate supply price" of that level of employment—where all variables are measured in wage units—are always precisely equal to the quantity of employment being considered.

It should be emphasized that this conclusion follows directly from the definition of "measurement in terms of wage units"—which means that the values of the variables are measured in terms of the quantities of labor which they respectively represent. It is *not* based on the assumption that the wage unit is constant. On the other hand, if such an assumption were to be added to the preceding ones, then —in Keynes' concluding words in the aforementioned note—"the aggregate supply function [which now refers to Z, and not Z_w] is linear with a slope given by the reciprocal[8] of the money-wage."

---

employ an additional quantity of labor, and not the additional proceeds that they actually expect.

8. Either this word should not appear here, or else it refers to the measurement of the slope with respect to the vertical axis.

In Fig. 9.1 I have also indicated the level of full employment N_F and have assumed that under no circumstances are workers willing to exceed this level. This assumption is reflected by the fact that the supply curve becomes vertical at this point. In this way the diagram can also be used to illustrate Keynes' interpretation of Say's law "that the aggregate demand price of output as a whole is equal to its aggregate supply price for all volumes of output, . . . [so] that there is no obstacle to full employment" (GT p. 26). That is, under the assumption of Say's law the demand curve $f(N)$ becomes a 45° radius-vector extending indefinitely rightwards, thus coinciding with the supply curve $\phi(N)$ until the point of full employment N_F.[9]

It should, however, be noted that Keynes does not explain here the nature of the dynamic mechanism which brings the economy to the point of full employment. Nor does he provide such an explanation when he returns a few pages later to the case of Say's law and writes:

On the classical theory, according to which $D = \phi(N)$ for *all* values of N, the volume of employment is in neutral equilibrium for all values of N less than its maximum value; so that the forces of competition between entrepreneurs may be expected to push it to this maximum value. Only at this point, on the classical theory, can there be stable equilibrium [GT p. 29; italics in original].

That is, Keynes does not explain here how "the forces of competition" generate full employment in this case. This, I would contend, is another manifestation of the deficiencies in the dynamic analysis of the *General Theory* to which I shall turn in a moment.[10]

As the reader has undoubtedly noted, the foregoing discussion also provides a rationalization for the standard diagonal-cross diagram, in which the horizontal axis represents not labor, but income measured in wage units. This is again represented by Fig. 9.1, where

9. I might note that Keynes actually misinterprets the passage from John Stuart Mill (1909, pp. 557–58) on which he claims to base this interpretation of Say's law (GT p. 18); for this passage is really nothing more than an expression of the innocuous "national income equals national product" identity! For details, see my *Money, Interest, and Prices*, Supplementary Note L.

10. Note also Keynes' imprecise use of the term "neutral equilibrium", for if the "forces of competition" push the level of employment upwards from any level of employment less than its "maximum value," then (strictly speaking) any such level is not an equilibrium one. In this context one might also note Keynes' later admission to Kaldor (in their correspondence of October 1937) that he had the "habit" of using the term "neutral equilibrium" when he meant "unstable equilibrium" (*JMK* XIV, p. 242).

the relevant symbols are now those in the square brackets. For once again the 45° radius-vector represents the aggregate supply price in Keynes' sense of the term: the minimum proceeds (measured as a quantity of labor) on which firms will insist in order to produce any specified aggregate output (again measured as a quantity of labor). For clearly the aggregate supply price of (say) the output OY_{w1} so measured is precisely the equal quantity OA so measured.

Despite the attention that I have devoted to Fig. 9.1, let me now emphasize that its failure to appear in Chapter 3 of the *General Theory* is not the sole or even a major source of the difficulties in fully understanding the theory of effective demand there presented. On the contrary, there are some basic difficulties in this presentation whose existence is even highlighted by such a diagram! Thus consider in Fig. 9.1 the level of employment N_1, or the resulting level of output Y_{w1}. The corresponding ordinate OA then represents the *actual* costs of production of that output. In contrast, the ordinate OB represents not the *actual* proceeds, but the *expected* ones. Why, then (as I think, Hawtrey kept on asking Keynes even before publication of the *General Theory*) does Keynes treat the difference between OA and OB as if it represented actual, realized profits that motivate the entrepreneur to expand output? And even more puzzling, why does Keynes contend that profits are at a maximum at the point of intersection of his demand and supply curves, where profits as measured by the foregoing difference are zero?[11]

Again, Keynes (*GT* p. 27, quoted above) says that for simplicity he will first carry out the analysis on the assumption of a constant money-wage. Nothing, however, is said about the price level. Clearly, however, this cannot also be constant. For in his earlier discussion in Chapter 2 Keynes states that he accepts the "first postulate" of classical economics that—because of decreasing returns—"an increase in employment can only occur to the accompaniment of a decline in the rate of real wages" (*GT* p. 17). Hence if Keynes' theory of aggregate supply price of output is to be consistently integrated with his theory of demand for labor input, then (on the assumption of a constant money-wage) a necessary condition for the increased input of labor required for the upward movement along $Z_w = \phi(N)$ in Fig. 9.1 is that the price level continuously rise along this curve, so that the real wage rate continuously falls.

From an alternative viewpoint (on which Keynes subsequently elaborates in his Chapter 21, "The Theory of Prices"), as the input of

11. Cf., however, Millar (1972), pp. 604–7. Millar's discussion is also of relevance for what follows.

where "the entrepreneurs' expectation of profits will be maximised" (*GT* p. 25, quoted above) and suggest that these words should simply be deleted from the *General Theory*. At first sight, this may seem to be a rather highhanded way of dealing with a problem of textual exegesis that has rightfully troubled many scholars over many years. I would like, however, to attempt to justify this deletion on the following grounds. First, these troublesome words do not appear in the corresponding passages, respectively, of the three successive sets of galley proofs that were run off during the first half of 1935 (*JMK* XIV, pp. 370–71). Second, and more important, though Keynes thus inserted these words into the final form of the *General Theory*, he left them without proof, and did not reproduce the proof of his mid-1934 draft (whose invalidity has been demonstrated in the preceding chapter) that the point of unemployment equilibrium is one of maximum profits. Correspondingly, I would suggest that just as Keynes continued to omit this invalid proof, so should he have omitted the conclusion that he had attempted to base upon it (cf. above, p. 77).

May I add that it is with great reluctance that I suggest solving a problem of textual exegesis by disregarding part of the text. I do so nevertheless in this case not only because of the reasons indicated in the preceding paragraph, but also because I find this solution definitely preferable to the alternative one, which is to attempt to rationalize these words by attributing to Keynes an involved chain of complicated mathematical reasoning which is entirely out of keeping with his usual analytical style.

I conclude accordingly that Keynes actually bases the dynamic analysis of the *General Theory* on the simple assumption of the *Treatise* that the existence of profits (which Keynes identifies with an excess of the aggregate demand price over the aggregate supply price) causes entrepreneurs to expand output; and conversely for losses. In particular, it is on this assumption that Keynes relies in the *General Theory* in order to explain how the dynamic forces of the market bring an economy to a position of unemployment equilibrium corresponding to the point of intersection between the aggregate demand and supply curves. Now, this assumption of the *Treatise*, like all the analysis of that book, is not derived from the principle of profit maximization. Nevertheless, because (I conjecture) Keynes wanted to present his *General Theory* as a theory firmly based on the maximizing principle of marginal analysis, he yielded to the temptation to denote this point of intersection as one of maximum profits, even though he had not provided the economic rationale for so doing.

Before concluding this chapter I would like to comment further on two points. First, in connection with the discussion of the behavior of the price level as the economy moves along the aggregate supply function, note the similarities with—and differences from—the *Treatise*. In both cases, an increase in output is associated with an increase in per-unit cost of production, and hence in per-unit price. But whereas in the *Treatise* the increase in cost is due to an increase in the wage rate—output per unit of labor input (i.e., efficiency e in the fundamental equations in Chapter 4 above) remaining constant, in Chapter 3 of the *General Theory* it is due to a decrease in the marginal product of labor—the money wage rate remaining constant. This analytical difference in large part stems from the integration of monetary and value theory that Keynes undertook as one of his tasks in the *General Theory*—as contrasted with his narrow concept of monetary theory in the *Treatise*, which caused him to declare the theory of wages to be outside his terms of reference, and which accordingly precluded his even mentioning the marginal product of labor (*TM* I, p. 151; cf. p. 13 above).

Second, I have already noted that Keynes accepts the "first postulate of classical economics" (*GT* pp. 5, 17); that is, he assumes that the firms of the economy are always on their demand curve for labor as determined by the latter's diminishing marginal productivity, so that changes in the level of employment are necessarily accompanied by inverse changes in the real wage rate. But, as I have argued elsewhere, the planned labor inputs specified by this demand curve reflect the firms' profit-maximizing behavior on the assumption that at the designated real wages they will be able to sell in the market all of their correspondingly planned outputs. Why, then, should this curve continue to be relevant for a situation of disequilibrium in which, by definition, this assumption is not fulfilled? In brief, despite Keynes' declared objective of integrating monetary and value theory, he did not really develop a theory of the demand for labor consistent with the state of unemployment qua market disequilibrium that was his major concern in the *General Theory*.[16]

16. The reference in this paragraph is to chap. 13 (especially pp. 319–24) of my *Money, Interest, and Prices*. This also provides a largely intuitive and admittedly problematic attempt to make good the deficiency just noted in the text. See also my earlier article on the Keynesian supply function (1949), as well as the next chapter. In recent years, this problem of analyzing behavior in conditions of market disequilibrium has received increasing attention in the literature. See in particular the well-known contributions of Clower (1965), Leijonhufvud (1968), and Barro and Grossman (1971).

10. The conceptual framework of the *General Theory*: I[1]

A book, especially a great book, is far more than its component parts. It is a way of combining these parts into a conceptual framework—a vision, a way of looking at the world.[2]

What was the vision that Keynes presented in the *General Theory*? It started with an "antivision"—a rejection of the traditional view that there existed in the capitalist world an automatic, self-adjusting mechanism that could be relied upon to maintain an acceptable state of employment.

Some aspects of this view can already be seen in a document that Keynes prepared in 1930 for the Committee of Economists of the Economic Advisory Council. Because the relevant passage here brings out so sharply the dynamic framework within which Keynes carried out his analysis, I would like to quote it at length, even though its primary context (the balance-of-payments problem) is not that of the *General Theory*:

> In minimising in the past the importance of the transfer problem, we have, I think, had in mind a situation which was changing only slowly. In this event, the amount of the necessary rate of change in money wages would be small, so that (assuming progress) the mere lapse of a little time during which money wages were not raised would be enough. Moreover, there would always be time for modifications to have their ultimate effect, before anything very dreadful happened.
>
> The trouble today is that we are violently out of equilibrium, and that we cannot wait long enough for *laissez-faire* remedies to bring their reward. In particular, a reduction in money wages might at long last have a very beneficial effect on the value of our total exports; but it may be quite impossible for us greatly to increase our favourable balance quickly merely by reducing money wages.

1. I shall in this and the following chapter draw freely on my "Price Flexibility and Full Employment" (1951) and *Money, Interest, and Prices*, 1st ed. (1956) and 2d ed. (1965).
2. Cf. Schumpeter (1954), pp. 41–42, 561–62.

I suspect, therefore, that the correct answer on austere lines is as follows: A reduction of money wages by 10 per cent will ease unemployment in five years' time. In the meanwhile you must grin and bear it.

But if you can't grin and bear it, and are prepared to have some abandonment of *laissez-faire* by tariffs, import prohibitions, subsidies, government investment and deterrents to foreign lending, then you can hope to get straight sooner. You will also be richer in the sense of owning more capital goods and foreign investments five years hence. You may, moreover, have avoided a social catastrophe. But you may also have got into bad habits and ten years hence you may be a trifle worse off than if you had been able to grin and bear it.

The worst of all, however, will be an attempt to grin and bear it which fails to last through. The risk of this is perhaps the biggest argument against the "grin and bear it" policy [*JMK* XIII, pp. 198–99].

The theme that one cannot rely on what Keynes in the *General Theory* (p. 266) came to call "the self-adjusting quality of the economic system" is one that recurs throughout the process of developing that book. Thus in the 1931–32 draft, the first surviving one, we already find:

There are also, I should admit, forces which one might fairly well call "automatic" which operate under any normal monetary system in the direction of restoring a long-period equilibrium between saving and investment. The point upon which I cast doubt—though the contrary is generally believed—is whether these "automatic" forces will, in the absence of deliberate management, tend to bring about not only an equilibrium between saving and investment but also an optimum level of production [*JMK* XIII, p. 395].

Again, in the unpublished "Historical Retrospect" that he prepared in 1932, Keynes wrote:

The orthodox equilibrium theory of economics has assumed, or at least not denied, that there are natural forces tending to bring the volume of the community's output, and hence its real income, back to the optimum level whenever temporary forces have led it to depart from this level. But we have seen in the preceding chapters that the equilibrium level towards which output tends to return after temporary disturbances is not necessarily the optimum level, but depends on the strength of the forces in the community which tend towards saving. . . . it now seems to me that the economists, in their devotion to a theory of self-adjusting equilibrium, have been, on the whole, wrong in their practical advice and that the instincts of practical men have been, on the whole, the sounder [*JMK* XIII, p. 406].

And in his contribution to a BBC series in 1934, "Poverty in Plenty," Keynes gave a talk entitled "Is the Economic System Self-Adjusting?" in which he characterized as follows the differences of views that had been expressed by the various participants of the series:

I have said that we fall into two main groups. What is it that makes the cleavage which thus divides us? On the one side are those who believe that the existing economic system is, in the long run, a self-adjusting system, though with creaks and groans and jerks, and interrupted by time lags, outside interference and mistakes. . . . These authorities do not, of course, believe that the system is automatically or immediately self-adjusting. But they do believe that it has an inherent tendency towards self-adjustment, if it is not interfered with and if the action of change and chance is not too rapid.

On the other side of the gulf are those who reject the idea that the existing economic system is, in any significant sense, self-adjusting. They believe that the failure of effective demand to reach the full potentialities of supply, in spite of human psychological demand being immensely far from satisfied for the vast majority of individuals, is due to much more fundamental causes. . . .

The strength of the self-adjusting school depends on its having behind it almost the whole body of organised economic thinking and doctrine of the last hundred years. . . .

Now *I* range myself with the heretics. . . . There is, I am convinced, a fatal flaw in that part of the orthodox reasoning which deals with the theory of what determines the level of effective demand and the volume of aggregate employment; the flaw being largely due to the failure of the classical doctrine to develop a satisfactory theory of the rate of interest.

Now the school which believes in self-adjustment is, in fact, assuming that the rate of interest adjusts itself more or less automatically, so as to encourage just the right amount of production of capital goods to keep our incomes at the maximum level which our energies and our organisation and our knowledge of how to produce efficiently are capable of providing. This is, however, pure assumption. . . .

None of this, however, will happen by itself or of its own accord. The system is not self-adjusting, and, without purposive direction, it is incapable of translating our actual poverty into our potential plenty [*JMK* XIII, pp. 486–91; italics in original].

What was the positive side of Keynes' vision? What was the over-all conceptual framework that he constructed out of the three major analytical components that he saw in the *General Theory*—the theory of effective demand, the theory of liquidity preference, and the marginal efficiency of capital?

It was a vision of a world in which economic decisions are unavoidably based on highly uncertain expectations as to future developments. By definition, this is particularly true for decisions with respect to investment. Correspondingly, the level of investment in the economy is very unstable. This instability in turn generates an instability in the level of employment.

More specifically, the level of employment is determined by the interaction of demand and supply in two markets: that for goods (consumption *plus* investment) and that for money. Reference to such an interaction (albeit in a different context) can already be found in the *Treatise*, though not as systematically set out as in the *General Theory*, and without explicit recourse to a demand-and-supply equation for money. I suggested above (pp. 45, 50) that the reason for the failure to carry out the exposition in terms of such an equation may lie in the fact that equilibrium in the market for goods in the *Treatise* was analyzed by means of an equation sui generis—the "fundamental equation." But once equilibrium in this market is analyzed (as it is in the *General Theory*) by means of an equation of demand and supply (even if it is of an unusual, aggregate kind), then one is naturally led to analyze the market for money by an equally systematic application of a demand-and-supply equation.

From this viewpoint, then, the *General Theory* can (as has been said more than once) be regarded as the first practical application of the Walrasian theory of general equilibrium. "Practical," not in the sense of empirical (though the *General Theory* did provide a major impetus to such empirical work), but in the sense of reducing Walras' formal model of n simultaneous equations in n unknowns to a manageable model from which implications for the real world could be drawn. Furthermore, though on this point it does not in principle differ from the model that Walras had developed in Lessons 29–30 of his *Elements of Pure Economics* (1900),[3] the model of the *General Theory* was one that integrated the real and monetary sectors of the economy.

At the same time, it seems to me highly unlikely that Keynes himself viewed his work in this simultaneous-equation way. The clearest evidence on this score is afforded by his contention that "definite error creeps into the classical theory [of interest]" when it determines the equilibrium rate of interest as the intersection point of the saving and investment curves, without taking account of the fact that the level of investment determines the level of income, which in turn determines the position of the savings curve (*GT* pp. 177–81). Harrod, in his fascinating correspondence with Keynes on this point during the summer of 1935, tried repeatedly to get Keynes to see that his criticism of the classical theory of interest was exaggerated: that this theory was not "in error," but that it was only necessary to replace its savings function by one dependent on income as well as interest, and then to determine simultaneously the equilibrium levels of both variables by also taking account of the liquidity-preference equation (*JMK* XIII, pp. 526–65, especially pp. 531–32, 545–46, and 553–54). But Keynes refused to accept this view. Instead, he continued to insist that a basic tenet of his theory was that savings and investment determined the level of income and *not* the rate of interest, whereas the rate of interest was instead determined by liquidity preference.

This tenet, indeed, served Keynes as a test of faith for all who wanted to be regarded as true converts to his new theory. I am overdramatizing somewhat: but this is surely the tone of Keynes' complaint to Harrod in a revealing letter to him of 27 August 1935 ("your acceptance of my constructive parts can only be partial if you do not accept my critical sections"), as well as the corresponding tone of the words with which Harrod hastened to reply ("No, no; you do me throughout great injustice. I have understood you much better than you think")—the reply in which Harrod explained his views in terms of the savings-investment diagram that Keynes later used on p. 180 of the *General Theory*. And this is again the tone in which, in the light of this explanation, Keynes then wrote to Harrod: "I absolve you completely of misunderstanding my theory" (*JMK* XIII, pp. 548, 553, 557). But despite the "absolution" he thus granted, and despite his adoption of Harrod's diagram, Keynes persisted to the published end with his contention that the classical theory of interest was guilty of "definite error" (*GT* p. 178).

3. See my *Money, Interest, and Prices*, Supplementary Note C.

Further evidence of a broader nature on the absence of a formal simultaneous-equation approach on the part of Keynes is provided by the logic of the way in which Keynes organized the argument of the *General Theory* into "Books." In Book I "Introduction," Keynes presents (in Chapter 3) a preliminary version of his theory of effective demand, and in this context identifies the consumption and investment functions as the two components that make up the aggregate demand function. Then (after devoting Book II to "a digression," "Definition and Ideas") he proceeds to devote Books III and IV—"The Propensity to Consume" and "The Inducement to Invest"—to a more detailed discussion of these two components. On the other hand, Keynes does not in a parallel fashion devote a "Book" to an exposition of his theory of liquidity preference. Instead, his discussion of liquidity preference appears in a group of chapters in Book IV (Chapters 13–15) which serve the purpose of determining the rate of interest that will prevail in the economy, and hence the specific point to which the economy's "inducement to invest" (which, as just noted, is the designated subject of Book IV) will be carried.

Thus to the extent that he thought in graphical terms, the picture that Keynes had before him was that of Fig. 9.1 above, which carries out the analysis in the market for commodities and then reflects the influence of the money market (via the rate of interest) by appropriate shifts in the investment (and hence aggregate demand) function; see the discussion of Fig. 10.1 below. It was not the Walrasian general-equilibrium IS-LM diagram, with its parallel treatment of the commodity and money markets.

This, of course, does not imply that Keynes objected to the IS-LM interpretation of the *General Theory* once Hicks had presented it in his famous "Mr. Keynes and the 'Classics' " (1937). On the contrary, after receiving an advanced draft of the paper from Hicks, Keynes wrote him (at the end of March 1937, just before the publication of the paper) saying that he "found it very interesting and really have next to nothing to say by way of criticism" (*JMK* XIV, p. 79). Nor did the criticisms which Keynes did have to make include any of Hicks's graphical interpretation.

In any event, Keynes' procedure in the *General Theory* provides another and more significant manifestation of the continued influences of the Marshallian way of thinking on him. For Keynes' procedure is basically the Marshallian partial-equilibrium one, which determines the equilibrium price and quantity in the market for any specific good by first analyzing the demand and supply curves in that market under the assumption of "other things equal," and which then takes account of the changes that may be generated in these "other things" as a result of interactions with other markets, by making appropriate shifts in the curves of the originally considered market.[4] At the same time I must emphasize that the interactions between markets play an incomparably more important role in Keynes' *General Theory* than in Marshall's *Principles*. From this viewpoint, then, I return to my original contention that the analysis of the *General Theory* is in effect a Walrasian, general-equilibrium one.

My conclusion from all this is that even if Keynes did in his own mind draw a sharp distinction between the Marshallian and Walrasian approaches to economic analysis (and I have serious doubts about that), he effectively made use of both of them in the *General Theory*. Correspondingly, I feel that Keynes would have had little understanding for and even less patience with any attempt to classify him as a strict adherent of one of these approaches to the exclusion of the other.

If we now take account of Keynes' "antivision" and supplement it with an understanding of the logical organization of the *General Theory* we can readily deal with one of the most debated issues of Keynesiology: Is the analysis of the *General Theory* based on the assumption of rigid or of flexible money wages?

The answer is straightforward. As we have seen, a major objective of the *General Theory* is to refute the classical view that there is an automatic market mechanism that assures the maintenance of full employment; the crucial component of this mechanism, that which sets it and keeps it in motion, is a decline in money wages in the face of unemployment; correspondingly, a major objective of the *General Theory* is to analyze the effects of such a decline and thereby show that it does not generate the results claimed for it. Conversely, if the *General Theory* were to be interpreted as being based on the assumption of absolute rigidity of money wages, then there would be no novelty to its message: for the fact that such a rigidity can generate unemployment was a commonplace of classical economics.

But in order to "facilitate the exposition"—and in accordance with the Marshallian procedure that he had adopted—Keynes first presents (in Book I of the *General Theory*) a "brief summary" of his

---

4. See, for example, Marshall's analysis of the effects of "a cheapening of the supply of a rival commodity" (*Principles*, 8th ed., p. 100) and of joint demand and supply (ibid., pp. 381–93). See also Keynes' description of the analytical procedure that he recommends for economists: "after we have reached a provisional conclusion by isolating the complicating factors one by one, we then have to go back on ourselves and allow, as well as we can, for the probable interactions of the factors amongst themselves. This is the nature of economic thinking" (*GT* p. 297).

theory on the simplifying assumption ("with which we shall dispense later") that money wages are constant (*GT* p. 27) and defers the fulfillment of the foregoing objective until Book V, "Money-Wages and Prices." And at the very beginning of this Book, in the opening paragraphs of Chapter 19, entitled "Changes in Money-Wages," Keynes once again explains the logic of his procedure:

> It would have been an advantage if the effects of a change in money-wages could have been discussed in an earlier chapter. For the classical theory has been accustomed to rest the supposedly self-adjusting character of the economic system on an assumed fluidity of money-wages; and, when there is rigidity, to lay on this rigidity the blame of maladjustment.
>
> It was not possible, however, to discuss this matter fully until our own theory had been developed. For the consequences of a change in money-wages are complicated. A reduction in money-wages is quite capable in certain circumstances of affording a stimulus to output, as the classical theory supposes. My difference from this theory is primarily a difference of analysis; so that it could not be set forth clearly until the reader was acquainted with my own method [*GT* p. 257].

As Keynes then goes on to explain, what his "method" demonstrates is that the primary way in which a decline in wages and prices can possibly stimulate the aggregate level of employment is by the increase that it generates in the real quantity of money—which in turn causes the rate of interest to fall, and hence the level of investment to rise. Hence, concludes Keynes,

> We can, therefore, theoretically at least, produce precisely the same effects on the rate of interest by reducing wages, whilst leaving the quantity of money unchanged, that we can produce by increasing the quantity of money whilst leaving the level of wages unchanged. It follows that wage reductions, as a method of securing full employment, are also subject to the same limitations as the method of increasing the quantity of money. The same reasons as those mentioned above, which limit the efficacy of increases in the quantity of money as a means of increasing investment to the optimum figure, apply *mutatis mutandis* to wage reductions. Just as a moderate increase in the quantity of money may exert an inadequate influence over the long-term rate of interest, whilst an immoderate increase may offset its other advantages by its disturbing effect on confidence; so a moderate reduction in money-wages may prove inadequate, whilst an im-

moderate reduction might shatter confidence even if it were practicable [*GT* pp. 266–67].

What specifically did Keynes have in mind when he referred here to the "reasons . . . mentioned above"? From the context, it would seem to have been to his discussion in Chapters 13 and 15 of the *General Theory* about those difficulties of reducing the long-term rate of interest that stem from what is effectively a high interest-elasticity of the demand for money (see especially *GT* pp. 172–73, 201–8); and to his discussion in Chapter 12 of the crucial influence of expectations on the investment schedule, which led him to the conclusion that "it seems likely that the fluctuations in the market estimation of the marginal efficiency of different types of capital . . . will be too great to be offset by any practicable changes in the rate of interest" (*GT* p. 164; see also pp. 148–49)—i.e., to the conclusion that the interest elasticity is not only effectively high with respect to the demand for money (which limits the "practicable changes" in this rate) but also (because of the aforementioned "fluctuations") effectively low with respect to the demand for investment goods.

I should note here that Keynes himself does not use the term "elasticity" in either of these discussion . Furthermore—and this is another characteristic of Keynes' analytical style—he frequently does not distinguish precisely, if at all, between the results due to the properties of a given demand curve and those due to a shift in the curve itself.[5] Thus when in the aforementioned discussion he argues that "circumstances can develop in which even a large increase in the quantity of money may exert a comparatively small influence on the rate of interest," he explains this by the fact that such an increase "may cause so much uncertainty about the future that liquidity-preferences due to the precautionary-motive may be strengthened" (*GT* p. 172). And it is Keynes' views on the combined effects of such shifts along and of the demand curves for money and investment goods, respectively, that have been denoted in the preceding paragraph by the term "effective elasticity."

Though it is only these effective elasticities which have operational implications for the analysis of the *General Theory*, it is worth asking what Keynes' views were with respect to the "pure" interest elasticity of investment—by which I mean the elasticity that would exist in the absence of the aforementioned expectational influences. Unfortunately, the *General Theory* does not provide a precise and unambiguous answer to this question. For example, the paragraph

5. For a contrary example see, however, p. 197 of the *General Theory*.

just preceding the one on p. 164 from which I have quoted above reads:

> Thus after giving full weight to the importance of the influence of short-period changes in the state of long-term expectation as distinct from changes in the rate of interest, we are still entitled to return to the latter as exercising, at any rate, in normal circumstances, a great, though not a decisive, influence on the rate of investment. Only experience, however, can show how far management of the rate of interest is capable of continuously stimulating the appropriate volume of investment [*GT* p. 164].

Does the "great, though not decisive" influence of the rate of interest on investment mean a high or low interest elasticity? A somewhat clearer implication that this elasticity is low seems to emerge from a later discussion in which Keynes writes:

> When there is a change in the prospective yield of capital or in the rate of interest, the schedule of the marginal efficiency of capital will be such that the change in new investment will not be in great disproportion to the change in the former [*GT* p. 250].

But this passage occurs in the context of Keynes' attempt to explain the observed relative stability of the real world; hence it might refer not to the pure interest elasticity, but to the effective one, as modified by the expectations which affect this reality.

What seems to me, however, clearly to indicate that Keynes of the *General Theory* believed that even the pure interest elasticity of investment is low is his contention that if investment at full employment could only be maintained, then the marginal efficiency of capital and hence the rate of interest would be brought down "approximately to zero within a single generation" (*GT* p. 220). In a similar context, Keynes writes in the final chapter of the *General Theory*:

> I feel sure that the demand for capital is strictly limited in the sense that it would not be difficult to increase the stock of capital up to a point where its marginal efficiency had fallen to a very low figure [*GT* p. 375].

Keynes then goes on to tell us once again that this situation could be achieved "within one or two generations" (p. 377). Needless to say, this view is not distinctively Keynesian, but has its antecedents in the classical notion of a stationary state. In any event, it is a view that should be contrasted with the one that was then being vigorously expounded by, say, Frank Knight, about the relatively high long-run interest elasticity of investment (Knight 1932, pp. 262–64; 1936, pp. 619–26).

Let me now return to the dynamic process described in Chapter 19 of the *General Theory* and note that in principle it is possible that this process will generate adverse expectations that will just exactly offset the otherwise stimulating effect on investment of the decline in interest. That is, there may be a special combination of circumstances which will prevent the decline in money wages from having any net effect on the level of aggregate demand. Under such circumstances, the equilibrium level of aggregate real output, hence the level of input of labor, hence the marginal product of labor, and hence the real wage rate will all remain unchanged. And I think that it is simply this special case that Keynes has in mind in that obscure, oft-cited passage in Chapter 2 of the *General Theory* in which he contends that "there may exist no expedient by which labour as a whole can reduce its *real* wage to a lower figure by making revised *money* bargains with the entrepreneurs" (*GT* p. 13; italics in original). This conjecture draws further support from the fact that at many points in Chapter 2 Keynes clearly has in mind the analysis to come in Chapter 19—as is evidenced by his repeated cross references to it (*GT* pp. 7, 8, 11, 12 n., 13 n., 18).

In accordance with his general analytical style, Keynes does not provide a graphical presentation of the argument of Chapter 19. This can, however, be readily done, as in Fig. 10.1, which, in keeping with the Marshallian partial-equilibrium spirit of the *General Theory* carries out the analysis in the market for commodities and reflects other influences by appropriate shifts in the aggregate demand curve of this market. Correspondingly, the function represented by this curve reflects the influence of both the rate of interest r and the state of expectations E. And I have taken the liberty of resuscitating Keynes' mid-1934 draft and introducing these variables explicitly into the function.[6]

The argument now proceeds along familiar lines. An initial position of full-employment equilibrium Q is disturbed by a sudden wave of adverse expectation (represented by the change from E_0 to E_1) which causes the investment schedule, and hence the aggregate demand curve, to shift downwards and thus bring the economy to the new equilibrium position R, which is a position of less-than-full employment. The resulting unemployment causes a decline in money

6. In this draft Keynes defines E as representing the state of long-term expectations, whereas in what follows I shall not so restrict it. See the discussion of this draft in Chapter 8 above (pp. 74–75).

106

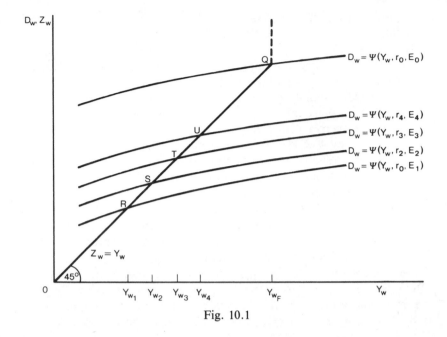

Fig. 10.1

wages, hence an increase in the real quantity of money, hence a decline in interest, hence an increase in investment, and hence an upward shift in the aggregate demand curve, thus bringing the economy to the new equilibrium position S. But since this too is a position of unemployment (even if less than that which prevailed at R), the wage decline and the dynamic process thereby generated continue, thus pushing the economy along the path T, U, . . . , which represents ever decreasing levels of unemployment. And the essence of Keynes' argument in Chapter 19 is that because of a relatively high interest elasticity of demand for money interacting with a relatively low interest elasticity of demand for investment—both of whose effective magnitudes are very much influenced by the state of expectations—this automatic adjustment process is not very efficacious: at best it can bring about only a very slow rate of improvement in the state of employment in the economy.[7]

Thus Chapter 19 of Book V is the apex of the *General Theory*. It is here that Keynes finally ties together all the elements of the analytical framework that he had developed in the Books I to IV in order rigorously to establish the *quaesitum* of his *General Theory*, namely,

7. In this context see also p. 173 of the *General Theory*.

There is, therefore, no ground for the belief that a flexible wage policy is capable of maintaining a state of continuous full employment;—any more than for the belief that an open-market monetary policy is capable, unaided, of achieving this result. The economic system cannot be made self-adjusting along these lines [*GT*, chap. 19, p. 267].

11.   The Conceptual Framework of the *General Theory*: II

There are several observations I would like to make about the interpretation presented in the preceding chapter. First, though it shows that Keynes did not assume money wages to be absolutely rigid, it obviously does not intend to depict him as going to the opposite extreme of assuming them to be perfectly flexible. Instead, Keynes' view of the real world was that "moderate changes in employment are not associated with very great changes in money-wages" (*GT* p. 251). At the same time, Keynes emphasizes that there exists an "asymmetry" between the respective degrees of upward and downward wage flexibility: that, in particular, "workers, are disposed to resist a reduction in their money-rewards, and that there is no corresponding motive to resist an increase" (*GT* p. 303). Similarly, there is an "asymmetry between inflation and deflation. For whilst a deflation of effective demand below the level required for full employment will diminish employment as well as prices,[1] an inflation of it above this level will merely affect prices" (*GT* p. 291).

In this context it is worth noting Keynes' description of what would happen if there were perfect wage flexibility. In Keynes' words,

> if competition between unemployed workers always led to a very great reduction of the money-wage, there would be a violent instability in the price-level. Moreover, there might be no position of stable equilibrium except in conditions consistent with full employment; since the wage-unit might have to fall without limit until it reached a point where the effect of the abundance of money in terms of the wage-unit on the rate of interest was sufficient to restore a level of full employment. At no other point could there be a resting-place [*GT* p. 253].[2]

1. Note that this does not necessarily mean that money wages also decline; see the discussion of the aggregate supply curve on p. 90 above.
2. Referring to this passage, Hawtrey (in his letter of April 1936) asked: "If by a reduction of wages wage policy can thus ensure full employment (even though it be only for a transitional period) can the unemployment which exists for want of such a reduction be called involuntary?" (*JMK* XIV, p. 31). Unfortunately for our purposes, Keynes did not reply to this question.

But Keynes apparently considered this conclusion to be as unrealistic as the assumption of perfect downward wage flexibility on which it was based.[3]

The question of workers' resistance to a reduction in money wages is also discussed by Keynes in his Chapter 2, "The Postulates of the Classical Economics." Here Keynes made his oft-cited statement:

> Whilst workers will usually resist a reduction of money-wages, it is not their practice to withdraw their labour whenever there is a rise in the price of wage-goods [*GT* p. 9].

On the basis of this statement, it is frequently contended that Keynes assumed that workers suffer from "money illusion." In the strict sense of the term, however, this is certainly not the case. Indeed, immediately after the foregoing statement Keynes himself explicitly rejects the contention "sometimes" made that this behavior is "illogical" (*GT* p. 9). And he refers the reader at this point to his discussion a few pages later in which he explains that workers

> who consent to a reduction of money-wages relatively to others, will suffer a *relative* reduction in real wages, which is a sufficient justification for them to resist it. On the other hand it would be impracticable to resist every reduction of real wages, due to a change in the purchasing-power of money which affects all workers alike [*GT* p. 14; italics in original].

In brief, Keynes assumes that the labor supply function of a worker depends not only on his own real wage, but on those of other

3. Variations on the foregoing passage occur at two other points in the *General Theory*, and at each of them Keynes mentions certain limits that the dynamic process might run up against before it could reach full employment. Thus when he describes this process in his appendix on Ricardo, Keynes states that "there will, it is true, be only two possible long-period positions—full employment and the level of employment corresponding to the rate of interest at which liquidity-preference becomes absolute (in the event of this being less than full employment)" (*GT* p. 191). On the other hand, in his Chap. 21, "The Theory of Prices", immediately after the passage on the "asymmetry" of wage behavior just cited in the text, Keynes writes: "If, on the contrary, money-wages were to fall without limit whenever there was a tendency for less than full employment, the asymmetry would, indeed, disappear. But in that case there would be no resting-place below full employment until either the rate of interest was incapable of falling further or wages were zero. In fact we must have *some* factor, the value of which in terms of money is, if not fixed, at least sticky, to give us any stability of values in a monetary system" (*GT* pp. 303–4; italics in original). In connection with the discussion of the "liquidity trap" that follows, I would say that Keynes considered all three of these theoretically possible outcomes (viz., full employment achieved by wage reductions, or a state of "absolute liquidity," or zero money wages) to be equally unrelated to the real world that he was analyzing.

workers as well. Hence the worker reacts in the differential manner just described. On the other hand, Keynes' assumption implies that the worker will react in exactly the same way to either a "rise in the price of wage-goods" or a corresponding reduction in *all* the money wages that he considers relevant to his own behavior. And this is the true meaning of absence of money illusion.

Second, according to Keynes' dynamic process as described in the preceding chapter, the only way a decline in the money-wage rate stimulates aggregate demand is indirectly, through the fall in interest generated by the resulting increase in the real quantity of money. Though I do not think it would have changed his basic conclusions, Keynes does not take account of the possibility that the increase in the real quantity of money may also exert a direct wealth effect on the level of aggregate demand. In a long-run growth context, Keynes does recognize that a higher level of wealth in the form of physical capital will generate a lower propensity to save and thus a higher propensity to consume (*GT* p. 218); but he does not apply this reasoning to the higher level of real financial capital (i.e., real money balances) generated in the short run by a lower money-wage rate.[4]

At the same time, it should be noted that even in the short-run context Keynes does take account of the effect on aggregate demand of changes in financial wealth generated by changes in the rate of interest.[5] Thus he writes:

> Perhaps the most important influence, operating through changes in the rate of interest, on the readiness to spend out of a given income, depends on the effect of these changes on the appreciation or depreciatioń in the price of securities and other assets. For if a man is enjoying a windfall increment in the value of his capital, it is natural that his motives toward current spending should be strengthened, even though in terms of income his capital is worth no more than before; and weakened if he is suffering capital losses [*GT* p. 94].

Strictly speaking, however, what Keynes is describing here is a *capital-gains* effect, and not a *wealth* effect; i.e., the effect of a *change* in the level of wealth, and not the effect of the *level* of wealth itself. For there is nothing in the foregoing passage to indicate that Keynes is assuming that the higher level of "the value of capital" will

---

4. Cf. my *Money, Interest, and Prices*, Supplementary Note K:1.

5. This point has been much emphasized by Pesek and Saving (1967), pp. 16–17, and Leijonhufvud (1968), pp. 190–93, 325–26, all of whom cite the following passage from the *General Theory*.

continue to have an effect on the level of consumption even in periods subsequent to the one in which the "windfall increment" in this value occurs. But this is the meaning of the wealth effect.

These doubts about whether the foregoing passage really reflects recognition of the wealth effect in the strict sense of the term are reinforced when we take into account the context in which it appears. This is one in which Keynes is examining the "objective factors" other than net income which influence the consumption of a given period. Among these factors he then lists these:

> *Windfall changes in capital-values not allowed for in calculating net income*. These are of much more importance in modifying the propensity to consume, since they will bear no stable or regular relationship to the amount of income. The consumption of the wealth-owning class may be extremely susceptible to unforeseen changes in the money-value of its wealth. This should be classified amongst the major factors capable of causing short-period changes in the propensity to consume [*GT* pp. 92–93; italics in original].

And the capital-gains effect of a change in interest described in the above-cited passage from p. 94 is then presented as a case in point. Thus the passage just cited from pp. 92–93 serves the double purpose of showing, first, that it is the *change* in the money value of wealth that generates an effect on consumption; and, second, that this effect is a *short-period* one. Correspondingly, there is once again nothing in the passage to indicate that Keynes recognizes that the higher level of wealth will—in accordance with the wealth effect—exert a permanent upward influence on the level of consumption.[6]

All this, however, still leaves the puzzle of why Keynes in his analysis of the effect of a decline in the money-wage rate does not treat the resulting increase in the real value of money balances as a "capital gain" that affects consumption in a manner parallel to that of the capital-gains effect that he does take account of in the case of a decline in the rate of interest.[7]

The third observation that I would like to make about the interpretation of the preceding chapter is that though it attributes to Keynes a belief in a high interest elasticity of demand for money, it does not

---

6. See also the similar statement that people "who take an active interest in their stock exchange investments . . . are, perhaps, even more influenced in their readiness to spend by *rises* and *falls* in the value of their investments than by the state of their income" (*GT* p. 319; italics added).

7. Cf. Patinkin "Money and Wealth" (1969), p. 1158.

attribute to him the belief that *the actual situation he was then analyzing* was characterized by an infinitely high one, what Keynes denoted as a situation of "absolute liquidity preference" (and what the subsequent literature has denoted as the "liquidity trap"). For Keynes explicitly states that "whilst this limiting case might become practically important in future, I know of no example of it hitherto" (*GT* p. 207). Similarly, at a later point Keynes states that (under certain assumptions) "conditions where the rate of interest can fall no further under *laissez-faire*, may soon be realised in actual experience" (*GT* p. 219)—which again indicates that to his mind this was only a theoretical possibility that had not yet been realized.

Yet there seems to be some ambivalence on this point in the *General Theory*, and there is even one passage in which Keynes seems to attribute "the acuteness and the peculiarity of our contemporary problem" of unemployment to "the possibility" that the economy had actually reached "the minimum rate of interest acceptable to the generality of wealth-owners" (*GT* p. 309). This isolated passage may simply have to be regarded as one of the inconsistencies that mars the *General Theory*. In the spirit of textual analysis, however, I would like to conjecture that this passage is a vestigial remnant of a view which Keynes actually held at an early stage of his work on the *General Theory*, and which he subsequently revised (along the lines of the passages cited in the preceding paragraph) under the impact of the continuous decline to unprecedented lows that took place in the long-term rate of interest in Great Britain throughout the period while Keynes was engaged in writing the *General Theory* (Fig. 2.1 above). Thus it is significant that it is precisely to this experience that Keynes refers in support of his "comforting hope" that the

> conventional and fairly stable long-term rate of interest . . . will not be always unduly resistant to a modest measure of persistence and consistency of purpose by the monetary authority. Public opinion can be fairly rapidly accustomed to a modest fall in the rate of interest and the conventional expectation of the future may be modified accordingly; thus preparing the way for a further movement—up to a point [*GT* p. 204].

Unfortunately, those parts of the earlier drafts of the *General Theory* which deal with the theory of liquidity preference and might have provided a test for this conjecture have not survived. I might, however, mention that in Bryce's notes of Keynes' lecture of 4 December 1933 there is a discussion of the problems created by a minimum rate of interest which is followed by the statement that

"K.'s belief is we have reached some such thing." On the other hand, there is no reference whatsoever to such problems in Bryce's notes of either the 1932 or the 1934 lectures.

Insofar as later material is concerned, this shows Keynes on the eve of the publication of the *General Theory*, rejecting as "extremely remote from [his] theory" Hawtrey's attempt to interpret Keynes' argument in terms of the possibility that the rate of interest "may get stuck for an indefinite period above (but not below) that correspond-ing to equilibrium."[8] It is also significant that there is no further reference to the "state of absolute liquidity preference" in any of Keynes' contributions to the intensive debate on the theory of in-terest that was later generated by the publication of the *General Theory (JMK* XIV, pp. 101–8, 109–123, and 201–23).[9]

My final observation on the preceding chapter is that I have inter-preted the *General Theory*, not as a static theory of unemployment equilibrium, but as a dynamic theory of unemployment *dis*equi-librium. More specifically, what concerns Keynes according to this interpretation is not an economy whose rate of interest, and hence level of employment, remain constant over time; it is instead an economy whose money-wage level and rate of interest are continu-ously falling, but whose "schedule of the marginal efficiency of capi-tal is falling more rapidly than the rate of interest" (*GT* p. 173),[10] thus

8. See the correspondence from Dec. 1935 reproduced in *JMK* XIII, pp. 621 and 631; see also *JMK* XIV, pp. 5–6, 30–31. See also Keynes' letter to Joan Robinson from November 1936 reproduced in *JMK* XIV, p. 141.

9. It is also noteworthy that the "liquidity trap" does not appear in any of the reviews and/or expositions of the *General Theory* that were published either by those who had worked closely with Keynes in the process of developing the *General Theory*, or by former students who had heard him lecture on the material of the book during this period. In the former category, see Harrod (1937) and Joan Robinson (1937), as well as Keynes' approving comments on these expositions (*JMK* XIV, pp. 83–86, 148–50); in the latter, see Champernowne (1936) and Reddaway (1936), who were "two former supervision pupils" of Keynes (*JMK* XIV, p. 59); see also the "very well done" which Keynes accorded Reddaway's review (*JMK* XIV, p. 70).

The origin of the "liquidity trap" (though in a notably less extreme form than that which later became the standard one of macroeconomic textbooks) is, instead, to be found in the famous 1937 article by Hicks, who was not a member of Keynes' immediate circle (see Hicks 1973, pp. 7–8). I must, however, admit that Keynes did not object to this part of Hicks's review in the letter that he wrote him on it (*JMK* XIV, pp. 79–81). See also my recent paper on "The Role of the 'Liquidity Trap' in Keynesian Eco-nomics" (1974).

10. See also Keynes' later description of unemployment as resulting from a situation in which the "rate of interest declines more slowly as output increases, than the marginal efficiencies of capital-assets" (*GT* p. 236). Though I have to a certain extent taken this passage out of its context, I do not think I am misapplying it. (There is a printing error in this passage in the new edition: "more closely" instead of "more slowly.")

generating a chronic state of unemployment, though one whose intensity is changing over time. In Keynes' words,

> it is an outstanding characteristic of the economic system in which we live that, whilst it is subject to severe fluctuations in respect of output and employment, it is not violently unstable. Indeed it seems capable of remaining in a chronic condition of sub-normal activity for a considerable period without any marked tendency either towards recovery or towards complete collapse. Moreover, the evidence indicates that full, or even approximately full, employment is of rare and short-lived occurrence. Fluctuations may start briskly but seem to wear themselves out before they have proceeded to great extremes, and an intermediate situation which is neither desperate nor satisfactory is our normal lot [*GT* pp. 249–50].[11]

My reason for emphasizing that this "chronic condition of sub-normal activity" is not, strictly speaking, one of "unemployment equilibrium" is my impression that it is precisely the mistaken tendency to view it in these terms that has encouraged the persistent attempts to interpret the *General Theory* (despite the internal evidence to the contrary) as being based on the special assumption of absolutely rigid money wages or (alternatively) the "liquidity trap." For (so the argument goes), by definition there cannot be a state of "unemployment equilibrium" unless wages are rigid. Alternatively, if money wages are flexible, then a necessary condition for equilibrium—in the sense of the level of unemployment remaining constant over time—is that the rate of interest remain constant; and a necessary condition for the rate of interest to remain constant in the face of an ever-declining wage level is that the economy be caught in the "liquidity trap."

Correspondingly, once we recognize that the *General Theory* is concerned, strictly speaking, with a situation of unemployment disequilibrium, we also understand that the validity of its analysis does not depend on the existence of either one of these special assumptions.

But how can I interpret the *General Theory* in this way in the face of Keynes' repeated statements that one of his major accomplishments in this book was to have demonstrated the possible existence of "unemployment equilibrium"? There are two—not mutually

11. See also Keynes' statement that the rate of interest "may fluctuate for decades about a level which is chronically too high for full employment" (*GT* p. 204).

exclusive—answers that I would like to offer: one dealing with style, the other with terminology.

Insofar as Keynes' style is concerned, let me refer again to that revealing August 1935 letter to Harrod (above, p. 99) in which Keynes also replied to Harrod's repeated criticism (*JMK* XIII, pp. 530–31, 535–37, 546) that Keynes' discussions of the classical position were carried out in an unduly polemical style that exaggerated the differences between the two positions. In Keynes' words,

> the general effect of your reaction . . . is to make me feel that my assault on the classical school ought to be intensified rather than abated. My motive is, of course, not in order to get read. But it may be needed in order to get understood. I am frightfully afraid of the tendency, of which I see some signs in you, to appear to accept my constructive part and to find some accommodation between this and deeply cherished views which would in fact only be possible if my constructive part has been partially misunderstood. That is to say, I expect a great deal of what I write to be water off a duck's back. I am certain that it will be water off a duck's back unless I am sufficiently strong in my criticism to force the classicals to make rejoinders. I *want*, so to speak, to raise a dust; because it is only out of the controversy that will arise that what I am saying will get understood [*JMK* XIII, p. 548; italics in original].

And what could "raise more dust" than a seemingly frontal attack on the "deeply cherished" classical proposition that there could not exist a state of unemployment equilibrium? Conversely, what could be more easily "accommodated" within the classical framework than the statement that a sharp decline in aggregate demand would, despite the resulting decline in the wage-unit, generate a prolonged period of disequilibrium which would be marked by a continuous state of unemployment?[12]

Insofar as terminology is concerned, let me again note Keynes' imprecise use of the term "equilibrium."[13] Similarly, I do not think that Keynes drew a sharp distinction in his own mind between static

12. That Keynes nevertheless felt apologetic about the highly controversial tone of the *General Theory* is clear from his preface to it (*GT* p. xxi). See also a presumably earlier draft of this preface, which deals at length with Keynes' views on the role of controversy in economics (*JMK* XIII, pp. 469–71), as well as Keynes' letter to Harrod from 30 Aug. 1936 (*JMK* XIV, pp. 84–85).

13. See above, p. 89, n.10.

equilibrium, on the one hand, and protracted dynamic disequilibrium, on the other.

Let me also note that though Fig. 10.1 as a whole describes a dynamic disequilibrium process, any point of intersection in it (say, point R) can indeed be said to represent an equilibrium position—for the short run. And this, I feel, is really all that Keynes meant when he referred to a "level of employment consistent with equilibrium" that is less than full employment (*GT* p. 28).[14]

All this comes out most clearly in the final chapter of Book IV —Chapter 18, "The General Theory of Employment Re-Stated"—in which Keynes summarizes the argument of his book up to that point. In this chapter Keynes defines his "dependent variables" as the levels of employment and national income, and his "independent variables" as "the propensity to consume, the schedule of marginal efficiency of capital, and the rate of interest." It is noteworthy, in connection with the discussion in Chapter 10 above about the Marshallian, partial-equilibrium character of Keynes' theory, that these three "independent variables" are precisely those that have to be kept in ceteris paribus in order to determine the position of the aggregate demand curve in Fig. 10.1.

Keynes then goes on to emphasize that the rate of interest itself is determined by the liquidity-preference function and the real quantity of money, so that the "ultimate independent variables" are the three behavior functions (consumption, investment, liquidity preference), the wage unit, and the nominal quantity of money. And it is by assuming all these constant that Keynes accomplishes his "present object [which] is to discover what determines *at any time*" the equilibrium levels of the dependent variables—employment, and hence output (*GT* p. 247; italics added).

But this is only a short-run equilibrium level. For, Keynes emphasizes, the "ultimate independent variables" are "capable of being subjected to further analysis, and are not, so to speak, our ultimate atomic independent elements" (*GT* p. 247). And in the following chapter—the crucial Chapter 19 on which the interpretation of the preceding chapter has been so largely based—Keynes does indeed subject the level of the wage unit to the "further analysis" whose results have already been described by the path R, T, U . . . in Fig. 10.1.

As further evidence that by the term "equilibrium" Keynes meant

14. I find support for this contention in the fact that Bryce's notes of Keynes' lecture of 29 October 1934 report Keynes as saying that the equilibrium determined by his theory of effective demand is one of "short period equilibrium only."

short-run equilibrium, I might also note that on the occasions that Keynes speaks of a position in which money wages no longer decline, or of a position (like that of the hypothetical "liquidity trap") in which their decline does not generate any further change in the level of employment, he does not use the term "equilibrium" unmodified. Instead, he uses the term "stable equilibrium" or "long-period position" or "resting-place."[15]

And may I now suggest that in all this there is yet another manifestation of Keynes' Marshallian upbringing! For surely there is an analogy between the point of short-run equilibrium R, initially generated by the decline in aggregate demand in Fig. 10.1, and the corresponding point of (in Marshall's terminology) "temporary equilibrium" generated by the decline in demand in Fig. 11.1. Similarly, there is an analogy between the successive equilibrium points T, U, V, . . . that are generated by an aggregate demand curve that shifts upwards in Fig. 10.1, in response to the resulting decline in wages and hence interest, and the corresponding equilibrium points generated in Fig. 11.1, first by the short-run supply curve S_1 corresponding to the

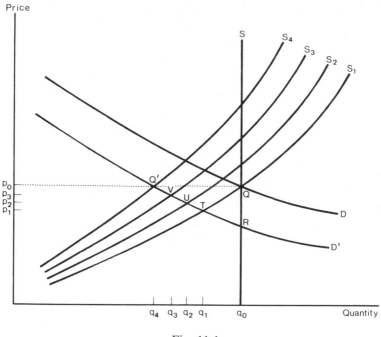

Fig. 11.1

15. See the passages cited in n.3 above and in the text to which it is attached.

existing number of firms in the industry, and then by the short-run supply curves $S_2, S_3, \ldots$, whose leftward shift reflects the exodus of firms from an industry suffering losses, as well as possible changes in factor costs. (Alternatively, and more in keeping with Marshall's exposition, this could be presented in terms of a shifting supply curve of different "runs," whose elasticity increases with the duration of the "run".) In the case of a constant-cost industry, this process ultimately leads to the reestablishment of a new long-run equilibrium position Q' at the original price level p_0 (Marshall, *Principles of Economics*, Book V, chaps. 2–3, 5).

But there are also important differences. First, whereas the equilibrating movement that brings us to the initial short-run position R in Fig. 10.1 is a movement in output, prices being held constant; that which brings us to the corresponding "temporary equilibrium" in Fig. 11.1 is a movement in price, output being held constant. This distinction has, of course, been much emphasized in recent years by Leijonhufvud (1968). It should however be stressed that it is a distinction that can validly be made only with respect to the process of reaching the initial short-run position R. Insofar as the subsequent dynamic process is concerned, it is clear from our discussion of Figs. 10.1 and 11.1 that it involves equilibrating movements of both price and output, in both the Marshallian and Keynesian frameworks. Correspondingly, I feel that the really significant difference between these analytical frameworks is that whereas Marshall's is a microeconomic one (which thereby enables him to ignore the possible repercussions of the dynamic adjustment process on the demand curve of the market he is, analyzing), Keynes' framework is a macroeconomic one (in which the adverse expectations and liquidity pressures generated by a contracting level of total output make it impossible to ignore such repercussions). It is this difference, and not the difference between price adjusting and quantity adjusting per se which generates the difference in the dynamic analysis. But it would take us too far afield to discuss this further here.

Second, whereas one of Marshall's primary concerns was to analyze the nature of the new long-run equilibrium position to which the industry in question would be brought as a result of the decline in demand, Keynes devoted little, if any, attention to the parallel question for the economy as a whole. Thus, he only incidentally mentioned the theoretical long-run position of full employment to which the economy might be brought on the unrealistic assumption of perfect downward wage flexibility. Instead, as has been contended above, what did concern Keynes was the dynamic situation of an economy in a state of unemployment disequilibrium, i.e., an economy which remains "in a chronic condition of sub-normal activity for a considerable period without any marked tendency either towards recovery or towards complete collapse" (*GT* p. 249).

Let me conclude this chapter with a few words on the eternal question of Keynes and the quantity theory. In the *Treatise*, as will be recalled, Keynes saw himself as providing a dynamic mechanism to supplement the quantity theory. In the *General Theory*, however, he saw himself as providing a new theory to replace it entirely. For, he claimed, the quantity theory holds only on two conditions: first, that the speculative demand for money "will always be zero in equilibrium"; second, that the level of output is constant at full employment (*GT* pp. 208–9).

As I have shown elsewhere (1965, chap. XII:1), the first of these conditions is not really a necessary one; for it actually stems from Keynes' implicit (and, I would conjecture, unintentional) assumption that there is money illusion in the speculative demand for money. The second condition, however, is obviously necessary. Hence in the world of changing levels of employment and output with which Keynes was concerned in the *General Theory*, there was no room for the proportionality of prices and money claimed by the quantity theory.

I would, however, like to conjecture that this change in view stemmed less from the shift per se from the analytical framework of the *Treatise* to that of the *General Theory* than from Keynes' changed outlook on the "normalcy" of full employment. For whereas Keynes of the *Treatise* still considered this as "normal," and thus analyzed the price movement from one position of full employment to another, Keynes of the *General Theory*—after five more years of even severer unemployment than that which had marked the period during which he wrote the *Treatise* (see Fig. 2.1 above)—was no longer willing to do so.

12. Theory and policy in Keynes' monetary thinking[1]

As indicated in Chapter 2 above, the changing nature of the policy problems that concerned Keynes during the interwar period can be read off the curves in Fig. 2.1, which describe the major economic developments of the period in the United Kingdom. Thus the problem of postwar inflation came and went. On the other hand, the problem that succeeded it—unemployment—persisted throughout the period and was accordingly Keynes' major concern not only in the *Treatise* and *General Theory* but to a large extent also in the *Tract*. I shall, then, largely restrict myself in this chapter to a discussion of Keynes' changing views on this problem as revealed by these books. In accordance with the scope of this essay as delimited in Chapter 1, however, I shall not attempt to supplement this discussion with a comprehensive analysis of Keynes' more politically oriented writings and activities, though I shall take account of some of them.

The empirical reality that stimulated Keynes' thinking on the problems of unemployment included the current developments in the United States as well as those in the United Kingdom. Correspondingly, it is important to note that, as can be seen from a comparison of Fig. 12.1 here with Fig. 2.1 in Chapter 2 above, these developments roughly paralleled one another, with the important exceptions that the period of protracted unemployment in the United States began about five years after it had begun in the United Kingdom, and that it was (unlike the case in the United Kingdom) associated with a sharp decline in money wages.[2] Note, however, that the onset of this unemployment in the United States was accompanied by a great intensification of its severity in the United Kingdom as well.

In order to provide a convenient framework for the following discussion, let me first summarize in a few oversimplified sentences the

1. This chapter has been significantly improved as a result of the valuable and stimulating comments on earlier drafts of it by Donald Moggridge and Donald Winch, to whom I am much indebted. I am also grateful to Susan Howson and Donald Winch for permitting me to refer to their forthcoming study on *The Economic Advisory Council: 1930–1939* (1976). Needless to say, none of these individuals is to be held responsible for the views expressed in this chapter. Indeed, with respect to some of these views there still remain some differences of opinion, or at least of emphasis.

2. The data for the U.S. refer to average hourly earnings, and are thus not strictly comparable with the British data on money wages depicted in Fig. 2.1. However, the difference between the respective rates of decline (7 percent for the U.K. during 1925–1933, as compared with 28 percent for the U.S. during the much shorter period 1929–1933) is far too great to be explained by this difference in definition.

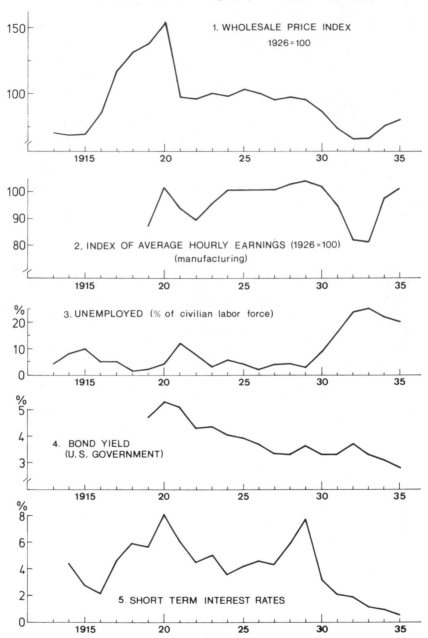

Fig. 12.1. Major economic developments in the United States, 1913–1935.
Source: U.S. Bureau of the Census, *Historical Statistics of the U.S.* (1960).
For chart 1, p. 116; for chart 2, p. 92; for chart 3, p. 73; for chart 4, p. 656;
and for chart 5, p. 654 (series 305).

familiar story of the development of Keynes' views on unemployment policy as they came to expression in his trilogy. In none of these books does Keynes advocate a policy of money-wage reductions as a means of combatting unemployment. Instead, in both the *Tract* and the *Treatise* he advocates the use of monetary policy for this purpose. Finally, in the *General Theory* he shifts his preference from monetary to fiscal policy. The realities that lie behind each of these sentences are, of course, much more complex—and it is to some of these complexities that I now turn.

Let me begin by tentatively suggesting that though both the *Treatise* and the *General Theory* reject the aforementioned policy of wage reductions, there is a nuance that separates them. In the *Treatise*, so I feel, Keynes believes in the theoretical validity of such a policy, but rejects it as impractical; in the *General Theory*, he does not even believe in its theoretical validity. More specifically, Keynes of the *Treatise* analyzes a reduction in money wages by means of his fundamental equations—and concludes that such a reduction would theoretically decrease the per-unit costs of production as represented by the first term of these equations, hence increase profits, and hence generate an expansion of output; nevertheless, in view of the great downward rigidity of money wages in the real world, Keynes rejects this policy as impractical and even damaging (*TM* I, pp. 241–46; II, pp. 162–65). In contrast, Keynes of the *General Theory* already rejects on theoretical grounds the "crude conclusion that a reduction in money-wages will increase employment 'because it reduces the cost of production' " (*GT* p. 261). In particular, he claims that this argument invalidly attempts to transfer to industry as a whole a proposition that is true for a single firm in isolation (*GT* pp. 257–60).

I might note that this interpretation of the *Treatise* helps explain another of its features: the fact that Keynes of the *Treatise* speaks almost enviously (and, I think, naively) of the greater ease (as it were) with which a totalitarian government can achieve a new equilibrium position that requires a reduction of the money wage per unit of output (or what Keynes called "the money rate of efficiency earnings"; see above, p. 34). In Keynes' words:

> It may be considered a defect that the central banking authority has in most modern economic systems no means of acting directly on the first term of the fundamental equation—that it cannot directly influence the level of efficiency earnings. In Bolshevist Russia or in Fascist Italy it may be possible *by decree* to change the money rate of efficiency earnings overnight. But no such method is available in the systems of capitalistic indi-

vidualism which prevail in most of the rest of the world (*TM* I, pp. 244–45; italics in original).[3]

And this is a recurrent theme of the *Treatise* (I, pp. 141, 151, 265, and 281).[4]

Might I also note that just as in the case with central-bank policy (*TM* II, p. 332), Keynes seems to express the belief that totalitarian policy, too, is more powerful in one direction than in the other! For in his discussion in the *Tract* of the inflation in Italy and its implications for the exchange rate of the lira, Keynes writes:

> In Italy, where sound economic views have much influence and which may be nearly ripe for currency reform, Signor Mussolini has threatened to raise the lira to its former value. Fortunately for the Italian taxpayer and Italian business, the lira does not listen even to a dictator and cannot be given castor oil [*Tract*, p. 119].

This last sentence is of course an allusion to the notorious force-feeding of castor oil by which Mussolini's fascists were then attempting to subdue their political opponents.

Let me turn now to Keynes' views on monetary policy. In the *Tract* (pp. 30ff) as well as in the *Treatise* Keynes considered the business cycle to be generated by alternations in the price level, with a rise in prices creating profits and hence encouraging the expansion of output, while a decline in prices had the opposite effect. Correspondingly, in the *Tract* (pp. 152 and elsewhere) as well as in the *Treatise* (II, pp. 189–90, 346, and elsewhere) Keynes advocated the same, basic policy for dealing with this problem, or at least mitigating its severity: namely, stabilizing the price level by means of appropriate variations (by the monetary authorities) in the rate of interest. As we shall see below, this apparent identity in policy proposals actually holds only for the case of a country for which international trade and/or finance is relatively unimportant. And even for such a country, there is an obvious and significant difference between the theoretical frameworks by which the *Tract* and *Treatise* respectively rationalized their proposals.

In the *Tract* (pp. 141–46), Keynes presented the following theoretical mechanism. A (say) lowering of the rate of interest would offset a

---

3. Note again Keynes' tendency, in the first sentence of this passage, to treat the terms of his fundamental equations as if they had an existence of their own (cf. p. 53 above).

4. Cf. also *JMK* XIII, p. 412. I must admit that this theme also appears in the *General Theory* (pp. 265, 267, and 269). Still, I feel that it plays less of a role there than in the *Treatise*.

downward movement in prices only by virtue of its first increasing the assets held by the monetary authorities (or what we call today the monetary base), hence increasing the quantity of money, and hence (by an implicit, mechanical application of the simple quantity theory) raising prices once again to their original level.

In contrast, Keynes bases the price-stabilization policy of his *Treatise* on the formidable analytical apparatus embodied in the "fundamental equations" that he there presents as his major theoretical contribution (see Chapter 4 above). Furthermore, he emphasizes that one of the distinguishing features of his theory as compared with that of Marshall (and Keynes could have added, though he does not, that of his own *Tract* as well) is that Marshall analyzed the influence of changes in the bank rate on prices only through their prior effect on the quantity of money; whereas Keynes' fundamental equations show that there is first a direct effect exerted through the influence of changes in the rate of interest on investment and saving (*TM* I, pp. 167–76). A related contrast between these two books is that whereas in the *Tract* it is the short-term rate of interest with which Keynes is primarily concerned, in the *Treatise* his ultimate concern is with the long-term rate, which is what influences the levels of investment and saving. At the same time, the major policy variable of the *Treatise* remains the short-term rate; for it is primarily through changes in this rate that Keynes proposes to affect the long-term one.

I should like to emphasize once again that in neither the *Tract* nor the *Treatise*, does Keynes regard price stability as an end in itself, but as a means of accomplishing the ultimate goal—stability of employment. This is a recurrent theme of the *Tract*: "All of us . . . are now primarily interested in preserving the stability of business, prices, and employment" (p. 138); "I regard the stability of prices, credit, and employment as of paramount importance" (p. 140); "the idea of utilizing bank rate as a means of keeping prices and employment steady [has] become practical politics" (p. 152); "the governors of the system would be bank-rate and Treasury bill policy, the objects of government would be stability of trade, prices, and employment" (p. 153). And what is true of the *Tract* is even more true of the *Treatise*, whose primary purpose (as we have seen in Chapter 4 above) is to construct a theory to analyze in detail the relationship between changes in the price level and employment, respectively.

Despite the operational equivalence of policy proposals[5] put forward in the *Tract* and *Treatise*, Keynes of the *Tract* seems to me to be more pragmatic and flexible in his approach, more aware of the

---

5. Albeit, only for a relatively closed economy; see below.

difficulties in the real world of determining precisely the appropriate times at which to make the interest-rate changes, and correspondingly more aware of the possible limitations of the price-stabilization policy. Thus he writes:

If the Bank of England, the Treasury and the Big Five were to adopt this policy [of stabilizing the internal price level], to what criteria should they look respectively in regulating bank rate, government borrowing, and trade advances? The first question is whether the criterion should be a precise, arithmetical formula or whether it should be sought in a general judgment of the situation based on all the available data. The pioneer of price stability as against exchange stability, Professor Irving Fisher, advocated the former in the shape of his "compensated dollar," which was to be automatically adjusted by reference to an index number of prices without any play of judgment or discretion. . . .

In any case, I doubt the wisdom and the practicability of a system so cut and dried. If we wait until a price movement is actually afoot before applying remedial measures, we may be too late. "It is not the *past* rise in prices but the *future* rise that has to be counteracted." [The footnote attached to this point in the text reads: "Hawtrey, *Monetary Reconstruction*, p. 105"] . . . .

As regards the criteria, other than the actual trend of prices, which should determine the action of the controlling authority, it is beyond the scope of this volume to deal adequately with the diagnosis and analysis of the credit cycle. The more deeply that our researches penetrate into this subject, the more accurately shall we understand the right time and method for controlling credit expansion by bank rate or otherwise. But in the meantime we have a considerable and growing body of general experience upon which those in authority can base their judgments. Actual price movements must of course provide the most important datum; but the state of employment, the volume of production, the effective demand for credit as felt by the banks, the rate of interest on investments of various types, the volume of new issues, the flow of cash into circulation, the statistics of foreign trade and the level of the exchanges must all be taken into account. The main point is that the *objective* of the authorities, pursued with such means as are at their command, should be the stability of prices" [*Tract*, pp. 147–49; italics in original].

In contrast, Keynes of the *Treatise* seems to me to be far more dogmatic in his advocacy of the policy of price stabilization—far more convinced of its infallibility and unquestioning about its practicability.

And I have the feeling that there is a direct relationship between the degree of scientism that Keynes attributed to his analytical apparatus and the degree of dogmatism with which—in these books, at least—he advocated his related policy proposal. Thus Keynes' simple, quantity-theory reasoning of the *Tract* led to the pragmatic, common-sense policy recommendations that have just been cited. On the other hand, the seemingly rigorous and scientific nature of Keynes' funda-mental equations led him in the *Treatise* to a far more doctrinaire and unqualified presentation of the price-stabilization policy. Such is the power and danger of a magic formula![6]

Thus, for example, while Keynes of the *Treatise* does mention some of the problems connected with the price-stabilization policy that he had discussed in the passage from the *Tract* cited above, he seems to attach less weight to them and to be fairly confident that they can be overcome (cf., e.g., *TM* II, pp. 189–90, 199–200, 305, 309–10, 313–15). In any event, I have not succeeded in finding in the *Treatise*, as contrasted with the *Tract*, any explicit recognition by Keynes that perhaps the monetary authority of a closed economy should be guided in its actions by additional variables besides the price level.

Again, when Keynes considers the possible limitations on central-bank policy that might arise in those circumstances "when, for a time, the natural rate of interest falls so low that there is a very wide and quite unusual gap between the ideas of borrowers and of lenders on long-term," his unhesitating answer is to call for ever more forceful central-bank action: to insist that we must under such cir-cumstances *"impose on the central bank the duty of purchasing bonds up to a price far beyond what it considers to be the long-period norm"* (*TM* II, p. 334; italics in original). For if the central bank does not do this, then the alternative is "allowing the slump to continue" or "socialistic action by which some official body steps into the shoes which the feet of the entrepreneurs are too cold to occupy" (*TM* II, p. 335). Furthermore, Keynes contends, "these extreme situations are not likely to arise except as the result of some previous mistake which has prevented the slumping tendency from being remedied at an ear-lier stage before so complete a lack of confidence had sapped the spirits and the energies of enterprise" (*TM* II, p. 335).

But things are not entirely as they seem to be; for despite Keynes' repeated expressions of unbounded confidence in the powers of

6. Other manifestations of this magic-formula mentality in the *Treatise* are discussed in Chapter 6 above. As we shall, however, see below, Keynes' doctrinairism in the *Treatise* is a more complex phenomenon than here indicated.

monetary policy to deal with the problem of unemployment, he concludes the applied-theory volume of the *Treatise* with a proviso that renders this policy inapplicable to the very England in which he was writing![7] In particular, toward the end of this volume (*TM* II, p. 335), Keynes notes that he has been "excluding so far from [his] purview" the presence of "international complications."[8] Such complications, he explains, arise from the fact that "no national central bank which is a member of an international system, not even the Federal Reserve System of the United States, can expect to preserve the stability of its price level [by means of variations in the bank rate], if it is acting in isolation and is not assisted by corresponding action on the part of other central banks" (*TM* II, p. 335). Keynes then goes on to say that

> it is the action of the lending countries of the world which mainly determines the market rate of interest and the volume of investment everywhere. Thus, if the chief lending countries would co-operate, they might do much to avoid the major investment disequilibria; that is to say, Great Britain, the United States and France. And if France prefers to live in a gilded grotto, Great Britain and the United States acting together could usually dominate the position [*TM* II, p. 337].

If, however, such cooperation is not forthcoming,

> there remains in reserve a weapon by which a country can partially rescue itself when its international disequilibrium is involving it in severe unemployment. In such an event open-market operations by the central bank intended to bring down the market rate of interest and stimulate investment may, by misadventure, stimulate foreign lending instead and so provoke an outward flow of gold on a larger scale than it can afford. In such a case it is not sufficient for the central authority to stand ready to lend—for the money may flow into the wrong hands—it must also stand ready to borrow. In other words, the Government must itself promote a programme of domestic investment. It may be a choice between employing labour to create capital wealth, which will yield less than the market rate of interest, or not em-

7. I am greatly indebted to Donald Moggridge and Donald Winch for having called my attention to the fact that I overlooked this important point in an earlier draft of this chapter, and as a result reached some erroneous conclusions.

8. I should note that there are also references to this proviso—though not to the "reserve weapon" which Keynes now describes—in the pure-theory volume of the *Treatise* (I, pp. 147–49, 242–47).

ploying it at all. If this is the position, the national interest, both immediate and prospective, will be promoted by choosing the first alternative. But if foreign borrowers are ready and eager, it will be impossible in a competitive open market to bring the rate down to the level appropriate to domestic investment. Thus the desired result can only be obtained through some method by which, in effect, the Government subsidises approved types of domestic investment or itself directs domestic schemes of capital development.

About the application of this method to the position of Great Britain in 1929–30 I have written much elsewhere,[9] and need not enlarge on it here. Assuming that it was not practicable, at least for a time, to bring costs down relatively to costs abroad sufficiently to increase the foreign balance by a large amount, then a policy of subsidising home investment by promoting (say) 3 per cent schemes of national development was a valid means of increasing both employment today and the national wealth hereafter. The only alternative remedy of immediate applicability, in such circumstances, was to subside foreign investment by the exclusion of foreign imports, so that the failure of increased exports to raise the foreign balance to the equilibrium level might be made good by diminishing the volume of imports [*TM* II, pp. 337–38].

Clearly, the greater the importance of international trade to the country in question, the greater the danger of loss of reserves. Thus the danger is greater for Great Britain than for the United States. (*TM* II, p. 336, n.1). Correspondingly, while (as we can see from the last paragraph of the foregoing passage) Keynes advocated a program of public-works expenditure for Britain, he continued (in his 1931 Harris Foundation lecture) to advocate the application of monetary policy for the United States (Moggridge and Howson, 1974, p. 236).

There are several comments I would like to make on the foregoing passage. First, perhaps because he took it for granted, Keynes barely mentions a further, crucial assumption of his argument: namely, "that it was not practicable, at least for a time, to bring costs down rela-

9. This is undoubtedly a reference (inter alia) to Keynes' famous May 1929 election pamphlet (written together with Hubert Henderson) on *Can Lloyd George Do It?: An Examination of the Liberal Pledge*. In this pamphlet, too, Keynes advocates public-works expenditures as a means of insuring that an expansion of credit by the Bank of England will be absorbed in the finance of domestic investment and will not simply lead to a loss of gold (*JMK* IX, pp. 118–19). This pamphlet will be discussed in greater detail below.

tively to costs abroad" (see the end of the passage). For if there were flexibility of prices and costs, then—as Keynes had demonstrated in the pure-theory volume of the *Treatise*—the same rate of interest that equilibrates saving and investment also equilibrates the balance of payments (*TM* I, pp. 191–93, 293ff).

In the absence of such flexibility, however, this is not the case. And the foregoing passage then reflects Keynes' application of the principle he had already enunciated in the pure-theory volume of the *Treatise*:[10] namely, that "with an international currency system, such as gold, the primary duty of a central bank is to preserve *external equilibrium*" (*TM* I, p. 147; italics in original; see also the specific reference to Britain on p. 148). Accordingly, Keynes assigns the rate of interest to achieving this goal, and calls upon public-works expenditure instead to achieve the goal of internal equilibrium (read: to increase employment).

Second, I would like to note that the distinction that Keynes implicitly makes in the foregoing passage between the respective effects on the balance of payments of a reduction of interest, on the one hand, and public-works expenditures, on the other, is tacitly based on the crucial assumption that the increased employment (and hence income) generated by public-works expenditures does not cause an increased demand for imports and thereby a worsening of the balance of payments. This tacit assumption also characterizes Keynes' 1929 analysis in *Can Lloyd George Do It?*[11] For Keynes supports his argument for public-works expenditure in this pamphlet with the contention that "an increase in effective purchasing power . . . would give a general stimulus to trade" (*JMK* IX, p. 106), and again fails to take account of the possibility that part of this "increase in effective purchasing power" would leak out into an increased demand for imports. It might also be noted that Keynes' argument here bears an interesting similarity to the one he had made in his famous 1929 debate with Ohlin on the German transfer problem. For in that debate, too, Keynes effectively ignored the influence on the demand for imports of the change in "buying power" generated by the German reparations.[12]

As is well known, the question of leakage into imports was shortly to be taken account of in Richard Kahn's famous 1931 multiplier article (pp. 11–15). But even before the appearance of this

10. Cf. n.8 above.
11. See n.9 above. The contention now to be cited is quoted at greater length below.
12. See Keynes (1929), Ohlin (1929), and the subsequent replies and rejoinders in the 1929 volume of the *Economic Journal*.

article[13]—and, indeed, even before the final publication of the
Treatise in October 1930—Keynes had recognized that such a leakage
exists. Apparently, however, he had neither the time nor patience to
introduce this point into the galleys of the *Treatise*—just as he did not
then have time to deal with Hawtrey's well-taken prepublication criticisms (*JMK* XIII, p. 139; see above, pp. 31–32).

In particular, in the "private evidence" that he gave before the
Macmillan Committee in March 1930, Keynes took account of the
fact that increased public investment would also lead to "the purchase of imports or goods which would otherwise have been ex-
ported" and hence "worsen the balance of trade."[14] This meant that
it would lead to a decrease in foreign investment, thereby generating
an "offset" to the stimulating effect of the initial increase in government home investment. It followed that the "*gross* amount of new
home investment has to be a sum in excess of the *net* additional total investment" that the government desires to carry out in order to
reduce unemployment (*ibid.*, italics in original).

Significantly enough, however, Keynes does not mention the fact
that the "worsening of the balance of trade" would also generate an
outflow of gold! It is as if in Keynes' mind gold flows were generated
in the balance of payments only by changes on capital account, and
not by those on current account. This is a puzzling point that deserves further study. In any event, it is clear that even in his evidence
before the Macmillan Committee, Keynes did not recognize that the
same reason (viz., danger of loss of gold reserves) which had dis-
suaded him in this evidence and elsewhere from recommending that
Britain should then lower the bank rate as a means of combatting

13. Which does not entirely rule out the possibility that Keynes' recognition of the
problem of leakage nevertheless stemmed from earlier discussions with Kahn. As Moggridge has, however, pointed out to me, this is not too likely in view of Kahn's
statement in recent years (1972, p. vii) that his multiplier article "was originally conceived in the late summer of 1930." Another possibility is that Keynes might have
become aware of the problem as a result of discussions with Colin Clark, who was
appointed to the staff of the Economic Advisory Council (of which Keynes was a
leading member) at the beginning of 1930, and who in June 1930 prepared a memorandum for the Council in which account was taken, inter alia, of the problem of import
leakage. In this context I might also note that it was Clark who provided Kahn with the
"statistical material" on which the latter based his pioneering estimate of the multiplier
(Kahn 1931, p. 13, n.4). Finally, there is the simplest possibility of all: that Keynes
became aware of this problem by himself! [My description of Clark's work has been
based on Howson and Winch 1976, chap. 3, especially nn. 22 and 57; see also *JMK*
XIII, p. 340.]

14. Committee on Finance and Industry (Macmillan Committee), unpublished minutes, 6 March 1930, p. 14 (in Keynes' Papers). Keynes "rashly ventured to guess the
proportion of the new investment that would directly or indirectly go to swell imports
as being of the order of 20 per cent at the outside" (ibid.).

unemployment, could also be adduced as an argument against the public-works expenditures which he recommended as an alternative.

My third and final observation on the long passage from the *Treatise*, pp. 127–28 above, is that though Keynes does provide in it a rationale for his preference for public-works expenditures in the case of international complications, I nevertheless find some incongruity in the fact that he should first devote his major analytical effort in the *Treatise* to establishing the truth of his fundamental equations and to demonstrating the crucial role that variations in the rate of interest play in bringing their respective "second terms" into equilibrium, and that he should then anticlimactically conclude that this analysis was not applicable to that country whose current policy problems were always his primary concern.

Perhaps Keynes, too, sensed such an incongruity, and perhaps it was this that caused him to be much less forceful in his advocacy of public-works expenditure in the *Treatise* than he had been in his joint pamphlet on *Can Lloyd George Do It?* Thus, for example, there is no mention in the *Treatise* of the incipient multiplier analysis with which Keynes had persuasively reinforced his argument in this pamphlet. In particular, in *Can Lloyd George Do It?* Keynes had contended that it was the "ABC of economic science" that "a demand for a suit of clothes implies a demand for cloth; that a demand for cloth implies a demand for yarns and tops, and so for wool,"[15] and, that accordingly "the indirect employment which schemes of capital expenditure would entail is far larger than the direct employment" (*JMK* IX, pp. 105–6). And to this, in a statement that is even more relevant for our present purposes, Keynes had added that

> the fact that many workpeople who are now unemployed would be receiving wages instead of unemployment pay would mean an increase in effective purchasing power which would give a general stimulus to trade. Moreover, the greater trade activity would make for further trade activity; for the forces of prosperity, like

15. Which, as indicated in Chapter 8 above (p. 71) raised the question of why an increase of one pound in expenditures on public works should not suffice to generate an infinite sequence of expenditures that would ultimately eliminte all the unemployment (cf. Lambert 1969, p. 246). The answer to this question was, of course, given by Kahn's subsequent analysis of leakages (1931, p. 13). As an indication of the state of the science just prior to Kahn's article, I might note that in the June 1930 memorandum which Colin Clark prepared (see n. 13 above), he intuitively rejected the possibility of "an infinite series of beneficial repercussions," but confessed that "the limiting factors [that determine the extent of the secondary employment] are obscure and economic theory cannot state the possibilities with precision" (as cited by Howson and Winch 1976, chap. 3, n. 22).

those of trade depression, work with a cumulative effect [*JMK* IX, p. 106].

Of all this there is not even a hint in the *Treatise*.[16] Nor can the omission be explained away on the grounds that Keynes (as he says at the end of the quotation from the *Treatise*, p. 128 above) felt no need to "enlarge" on what he had "written elsewhere." This would explain why Keynes chose not to repeat in a general *Treatise* the specific data and calculations relating to the British experience that he had presented in *Can Lloyd George Do It?* It does not explain Keynes' failure to reiterate a then-novel argument with general analytical implications of undoubted significance.

Perhaps it was also this sense of incongruity that lies behind what seems to me to be Keynes' subtle attempt to try to minimize the apparent difference between his policy recommendation in the foregoing passage and the usual one of the *Treatise*. In particular, Keynes tries to present his recommendation for government-stimulated investment as if it were effectively one for a reduction in the rate of interest, though a discriminatory reduction. That is, a reduction for domestic borrowers, who will be permitted to borrow at the subsidized rate of "(say) 3 per cent," but not for foreign borrowers, who will have to continue to pay the higher, market rate.[17]

I would now like to suggest that this incongruity is a manifestation of the simple fact that Keynes—like all of us—wrote and acted in different ways in the different roles that he played in life. In particu-

---

16. Is it another indication of ambivalence on the part of Keynes (or is there another, more mundane, explanation?) that the most persuasive passages from *Can Lloyd George Do It?* cited in the preceding paragraph were also deleted from the abbreviated form of this pamphlet which Keynes published, under the title "A Programme of Expansion (General Election, May 1929)," in his *Essays in Persuasion* (1931)? Or alternatively, might this be an indication that the deleted passages reflected more the views of Keynes' co-author, Hubert Henderson, than his own? Though I have for the sake of completeness listed this last alternative, I think that the available evidence must lead us to reject it. In particular, Harrod (1951, p. 395) tells us that "Keynes composed it [i.e., the original pamphlet] himself." Again, the editors of the new and enlarged edition of *Essays in Persuasion* have prefaced the reprinted pamphlet with the explanation that it "seems to have been, according to Hubert Henderson's widow, Lady Henderson, ' . . . a true work of collaboration about which there was never any question as to who gave the most' " (*JMK* IX, p. 86). Finally, it might be relevant to note that within less than a year after the publication of *Can Lloyd George Do It?*, Henderson had shifted his position and was expressing doubts to Keynes about the desirability of the public-works-expenditures policy they had jointly advocated. Indeed, in the 1930 and 1931 discussions in the Economic Advisory Council and Committee of Economists, Henderson vigorously opposed such expenditures, while Keynes continued to support them. See the fascinating account in Howson and Winch (1976), chap. 3, nn. 109–17, and the text to which they are attached.

17. Note, however, the similar presentation of public-works-expenditure policy a few years later in Pigou's *Theory of Employment* (1933), pp. 213–14.

lar, in his *Treatise on Money*, Keynes was the internationally famous scholar presenting to the scientific world as a whole what was intended to be the definitive work on the subject. Correspondingly, the policies he recommended in that work had an international orientation: in accordance with the universal truths enunciated by the fundamental equations, the solution to unemployment is, in general—and in the case of France and the United States at that time, in particular (*TM* I, p. 148)—to lower the interest rate: and if—as in the case of Great Britain at the time—this should create "international complications," such complications should be eliminated by appropriate international cooperation.

But even in an internationally oriented *Treatise*, Keynes could not completely escape the obligation to suggest remedies "of immediate applicability" to the current "position of Great Britain." And his pious hope for "international cooperation" was hardly such a remedy. Correspondingly, he added two brief paragraphs at the end of the long passage from the *Treatise* cited on pp. 127–28 above (and it is from these paragraphs that the foregoing quotations have been taken) to point out that in the event that such international cooperation should not be forthcoming, an economy like the British one could decide to go its own way and "partially rescue itself" by calling upon its "reserve weapon" of public works expenditures. Indeed, in this context Keynes was willing to depart so sharply from his international orientation as to add that "the only alternative remedy of immediate applicability, in such circumstances, was to subsidise foreign investment by the exclusion of foreign imports"—which, for reasons which will become clear in a moment, I interpret as a veiled suggestion to make use of tariffs.

But as we all know, Keynes was not only an internationally famous scholar, but also Britain's leading political economist, and one who played an extremely influential role in its public and governmental discussions of economic policy. And in this role his major concern was naturally with those policy proposals which were of immediate applicability to the British scene. Thus it was in this role that he wrote his *Can Lloyd George Do It*, urging the British voter to support the Liberal party program of public works expenditure. And it was also in this role that (inter alia) he continued to advocate such expenditures in his "private evidence" before the Macmillan Committee.[18] Indeed, in this evidence—and in other activities of his during the first half of 1930 and later—he even incurred the wrath of most of his

18. Committee on Finance and Industry, unpublished minutes, 6 March 1930 (in Keynes Papers).

academic colleagues by departing from the traditional free-trade doctrine of British economics and advocating the imposition of a revenue
tariff as a means of stimulating employment. Thus what Keynes was
willing only to hint at vaguely in his internationally-oriented *Treatise*,
he was beginning to advocate openly and with increasing vigor in the
domestic discussions in which he was then engaged.[19]

Before leaving this point, I would like to suggest that it may well
explain another incongruity in Keynes' behavior: the incongruity between the doctrinaire policy pronouncements of the *Treatise* to which
I have referred in this chapter (p. 126), and the fact[20] that in his
evidence before the Macmillan Committee, as well as in his other
writings and activities in the early 1930's, Keynes was anything but
doctrinaire, and was instead proposing a wide variety of policies to
deal with Britain's prolonged and even worsening unemployment.[21]
Once again, I think that the explanation for this difference lies in the
different roles that Keynes was then playing: that he tended to write
in a doctrinaire way in a *Treatise on Money* which he presented as the
definitive scientific work on the subject, and that he tended to adopt a
much more flexible and pragmatic approach in his testimony before
an *ad hoc* government committee charged with finding practical solu-
tions to the specific problems that then beset the nation.

As noted, the quotation from the *Treatise* on pp. 127–28 above
occurs at the end of the applied-theory volume of the *Treatise*. Actually, however, there is an earlier passage in this volume in which
Keynes also advocates public-works expenditures instead of a reduction in the interest rate. I am referring to Keynes' discussion in his
chapter on ''Historical Illustrations'' of his theory, where he indicates
that he would have advocated such expenditures during the period of
heavy unemployment that prevailed in Britain during the early 1890's.

19. For the details of Keynes' shift in view on the tariff question see Howson and
Winch (1976), chap. 3, especially n. 86. See also Winch (1969), pp. 150–51. The evidence before the Macmillan Committee in which Keynes first advocated tariffs was
presented on 28 February and 6 March 1930—at which time he was still revising the
galleys of the *Treatise* (*JMK* XIII, pp. 122–32).

Another possible indication of the different orientations of the *Treatise*, on the
one hand, and of the evidence before the Macmillan Committee, on the other, is the
fact that whereas in the *Treatise* Keynes gives pride of place to international cooperation as the means of solving international complications, in his evidence he mentions it
as the last possible remedy, after having expanded in detail on other remedies which
were dependent solely on domestic actions (Committee on Finance and Industry, unpublished testimony, 7 March 1930; in Keynes Papers).

20. Which was pointed out to me by both Donald Moggridge and Donald Winch; see
n. 1 above.

21. Indeed, such a variety that he was even criticized at the time for his ''fluctuating
views'' (Winch 1969, pp. 140–41).

In this context Keynes writes that "in the matter of bank rate it [the Bank of England] did what lay in its power to make credit easy." And even if it had then been possible to carry out open-market purchases (which in those days "had not been heard of"),

> consols were already at a high price, and it must be doubtful whether purchases of consols by the Bank of England would have done anything material to stimulate investment. It may have been a case where nothing but strenuous measures on the part of the Government could have been successful. Borrowing by the Government and other public bodies to finance large programmes of work on public utilities and Government guarantees on the lines of the recent Trade Facilities and Export Credit Acts were probably the only ways of absorbing current savings and so averting the heavy unemployment of 1892–5 [*TM* II, pp. 151–52].

There is no indication here that Keynes' advocacy of public-works expenditure in this case was motivated by the possible "international complications" that might have then been generated by a reduction in the interest rate. What does, however, seem to have influenced Keynes was his feeling that entrepreneurs in this period were so demoralized that no reduction in interest would have stimulated investment sufficiently.[22] In this context it is relevant to note that the years 1892–95 were part of what was, before the 1930's, known in England as the Great Depression (Mathias 1969, p. 395). I shall return to this point below.

Let me turn now to the policy views of the *General Theory*. As I have noted (p. 12 above), the major concern of this book is (as its title indicates) with theory, so that these views are not spelled out in great detail. Still, there can be no question as to what they were. In Keynes' words:

> For my own part I am now somewhat sceptical of the success of a merely monetary policy directed towards influencing the rate of interest. I expect to see the State, which is in a position to calculate the marginal efficiency of capital-goods on long views and on the basis of the general social advantage, taking an ever greater responsibility for directly organising investment; since it seems likely that the fluctuations in the market estimation of the marginal efficiency of different types of capital, calculated on the principles I have described above, will be too great to be offset by any practical changes in the rate of interest [*GT* p. 164].

22. See also the discussion on pp. 126–27 above.

Again,

> The State will have to exercise a guiding influence on the propensity to consume partly through its scheme of taxation, partly by fixing the rate of interest, and partly, perhaps, in other ways. Furthermore, it seems unlikely that the influence of banking policy on the rate of interest will be sufficient by itself to determine an optimum rate of investment. I conceive, therefore, that a somewhat comprehensive socialisation of investment will prove the only means of securing an approximation to full employment; though this need not exclude all manner of compromises and of devices by which public authority will cooperate with private initiative [*GT* p. 378].

This is the fundamental policy conclusion of the *General Theory* —the advocacy of direct government investment expenditures as a necessary means of assuring full employment. And this is also the policy difference between Keynes of the *General Theory* and Keynes of the *Treatise*; in the latter, Keynes tended to place much more reliance on interest-rate (monetary) policy as a means of achieving this end. It is, however, clear that these policy differences do not necessarily follow from the differences per se in the respective theoretical frameworks of these two books. For, as we have just seen, in the *Treatise*, too, Keynes—under certain circumstances—also advocated government investment expenditures.

But this very fact seems to me to provide conclusive evidence that a significant shift took place in Keynes' views on the efficacy of monetary policy between the *Treatise* and the *General Theory*. For, as we have also seen, Keynes of the *Treatise* advocated public-works expenditures for England instead of interest-rate reductions only because of his fears that the latter policy would cause a dangerous loss of gold reserves. But in September 1931 England abandoned the gold standard, and for several years afterwards effectively functioned as a closed economy.[23] Correspondingly, if Keynes had continued to believe in the supremacy of monetary policy, he should have welcomed this opportunity to reaffirm it; for this policy could now be carried out without fears of any possible "international complications"—i.e., possible adverse effects on the state of England's international monetary reserves. Now, it is true that such a reaffirmation did occur immediately after the devaluation. More specifically, in November 1931 Keynes wrote a memorandum for the Treasury which became

---

23. See Ashworth (1960, pp. 400 ff), A. E. Kahn (1946, chap. 10, esp. p. 179), and Youngson (1967, pp. 92–93, 126–27, 292–93). See also p. 16 above.

one of the bases of the subsequent cheap-money policy (Moggridge and Howson 1974, pp. 237–38). But this reaffirmation of faith did not last long, and within a relatively short time Keynes once again abandoned his belief in the efficacy of monetary policy in the circumstances that then prevailed.

In sum, I would conjecture that the difference between Keynes' policy views in the *Treatise* and in the *General Theory* stems less from the theoretical differences between these two books than from the experience of five additional years of unprecedented depression in England, during which the long-term rate of interest had continued unavailingly to decline (see Fig. 2.1 above). And I would also conjecture that Keynes' feelings on this score were only reinforced by the similar developments in the United States (see Fig. 12.1 above). It was this additional experience, I believe, that led Keynes to conclude that in the light of the overwhelmingly pessimistic expectations that then prevailed, no practicable reduction of the rate of interest would be great enough to encourage firms to increase their investments sufficiently to generate full employment. And it was accordingly this that ultimately brought Keynes to a decision to advocate for the Great Depression of the 1930's the public-works expenditures that he also felt would have been necessary for dealing adequately with the Great Depression of the 1890's.[24]

---

24. All this accords with the views that Keynes expressed in his *Means to Prosperity* (1933), a pamphlet which he issued in a U.S. as well as a British edition, and in which he addressed himself to the specific problem of unemployment that then beset both economies. In this pamphlet Keynes emphasizes that even after central-bank policy.has brought the economy to a "second stage . . . at which the long-term rate of interest is low for all reasonably sound borrowers"—a stage which "Great Britain alone has reached"—"there remains a third stage. For even when we have reached the second stage, it is unlikely that private enterprise will, on its own initiative, undertake new loan-expenditure on a sufficient scale. Business enterprise will not seek to expand until *after* profits have begun to recover. Increased working capital will not be required until *after* output is increasing. Moreover, in modern communities a very large proportion of our *normal* programmes of loan-expenditure are undertaken by public and semi-public bodies. The new loan-expenditure which trade and industry require in a year is comparatively small even in good times. Building, transport, and public utilities are responsible at all times for a very large proportion of current loan-expenditure.

"Thus the first step has to be taken on the initiative of public authority; and it probably has to be on a large scale and organised with determination, if it is to be sufficient to break the vicious circle and to stem the progressive deterioration, as firm after firm throws up the sponge and ceases to produce at a loss in the seemingly vain hope that perseverance will be rewarded" (*JMK* IX, pp. 353–54; italics in original).

13.   After the *General Theory*

The *General Theory* was finally published in February 1936 and was immediately honored with review articles by the leading economists of both the older and younger generations. Some of these reviews were written by individuals who had been directly or indirectly connected with Keynes during the period that he was working on the *General Theory*. In this category are to be found the detailed critique that Ralph Hawtrey published in his *Capital and Employment* (1937), as well as Roy Harrod's review in *Econometrica* (1937), which led to the revealing correspondence with Keynes that has been cited above in Chapter 8. There were also review articles by D. G. Champernowne (1936) and W. B. Reddaway (1936), two former supervision pupils of Keynes' (*JMK* XIV, p. 59). Similarly, there was a review article by a then-young instructor at the London School of Economics, Abba Lerner (1936), who had earlier been involved in a long series of discussions with some of Keynes' junior colleagues and with Joan Robinson in particular (*JMK* XIV, p. 148, n. 1).

Going outside Keynes' immediate circle, we have A. C. Pigou's sharply critical review in *Economica* (1936).[1] There were also the two reviews by John Hicks—first in the pages of the *Economic Journal* (1936),[2] and then his most influential "Mr. Keynes and the 'Classics' " in *Econometrica* (1937). Again, the *Quarterly Journal of Economics* devoted most of its November 1936 issue to a memorable

1. This sharpness stemmed primarily from Pigou's justified feeling that in order to "win attention" for his *General Theory*, Keynes had presented the ideas of this book "in a matrix of sarcastic comment upon other people" (1936, p. 115). In particular, Pigou deeply resented what he considered to be Keynes' serious misrepresentation of Pigou's own views, and even more those of Keynes' "old master," Marshall. More than a decade later, a few years after Keynes' death, Pigou returned to discuss *Keynes's 'General Theory': A Retrospective View* (1950). Here Pigou barely refers to the polemical aspects of the book that so offended him in his original review. And though Pigou still advances many substantive criticisms of specific points in Keynes' theory of unemployment, he concludes with the statement that "nobody before him, so far as I know, had brought all the relevant factors, real and monetary at once, together in a single formal scheme, through which their interplay could be coherently investigated." Pigou also admits that "in my original review-article on the *General Theory* I failed to grasp its significance [i.e., the significance of the single formal scheme] and did not assign to Keynes the credit due for it" (1950, p. 65; see also p. 20).

2. On the background of the invitation by the *Journal* to write this review, see Hicks's recent "Recollections and Documents" (1973), p. 8.

symposium in which Jacob Viner, Dennis Robertson, Wassily Leontief, and Frank Taussig each reviewed different aspects of the book. Similarly, many pages of the *Economic Journal* during 1937 were devoted to discussions of the *General Theory*. The most important contribution here was Bertil Ohlin's fruitful comparison of Keynes' approach with that of the Stockholm school—one aspect of which was a valuable sharpening of the distinction between planned (ex ante) and actual (ex post) quantities, a distinction which was always dangerously fuzzy in Keynes' writings (see pp. 73 and 90 above).

In one way or another, Keynes reacted to practically all of these reviews. These reactions (which are reproduced in *JMK* XIV) varied from brief discussions carried out only by means of correspondence (as in the case of Harrod and Reddaway) to published replies that were in many cases both preceded and followed by protracted correspondence (as in the case of Hawtrey, Robertson, and Ohlin). I shall not in this essay attempt to provide a detailed study of these exchanges, but shall instead be content with a few, brief remarks.[3]

Let me first say that having been formed and reformed in the fires of the detailed criticisms that Keynes solicited at every stage of its development, the *General Theory* stood up most successfully under the criticisms that followed its appearance. And this (as the reader will recall) was in sharp contrast with what had happened with the *Treatise*, both before and after publication. There were indeed some less integral parts of the *General Theory*—for example, the attempt at formal rigor in Chapter 17, "The Essential Properties of Interest and Money"—which proved to be deficient. Ohlin's comments were also well-taken. Still, the basic structure of the book not only remained intact, but also defined the framework of both theoretical and empirical research in macroeconomics for decades to come—truly a scientific achievement of the first order.

An immediate and natural corollary of this achievement was that in his replies to the aforementioned criticisms, Keynes felt no need to make any basic modifications or improvements in the analysis of the *General Theory*; nor did he do so. As just indicated, however, I feel that there was one criticism that should have stimulated such an improvement, namely, that implicit in Ohlin's articles. But instead of undertaking the fruitful task (that was to be carried out by the later

---

3. I shall also not deal here with the relevant criticisms then made of various empirical aspects of the *General Theory* by Simon Kuznets, John Dunlop, and Lorie Tarshis. Keynes' replies to these criticisms are reproduced in Appendices 2 and 3 of the new edition of the *General Theory*. See, however, my forthcoming "Keynes and Econometrics" (1976) for a discussion of some aspects of his exchange with Kuznets.

literature) of applying Ohlin's ex ante/ex post analysis to the theory of effective demand and to its dynamic aspects in particular,[4] Keynes devoted himself almost exclusively to its implications for the theory of liquidity preference—and in that context then began the pointless and depressing "liquidity-preference *versus* loanable-funds" debate that was to drag on in the literature for years.[5] This debate—which Keynes also carried on with Robertson—stemmed largely from Keynes' failure to adopt the appropriate general-equilibrium view of his own theory (see above, pp. 63 and 99).[6]

The corollary stated at the beginning of the preceding paragraph also applies to Keynes' oft-cited 1937 reply to the aforementioned *Quarterly Journal of Economics* symposium. This reply[7] actually pays little attention to the specific criticisms that had been made in

4. Note, however, that in Keynes' first reaction to Ohlin's manuscript, he stated (in a letter dated 21 January 1937): "As regards the *ex post* and the *ex ante* method, I shall certainly give further thought to its advantages. This is in fact almost precisely on the lines that I was thinking and lecturing somewhere about 1931 and 1932, and subsequently abandoned. My reason for giving it up was owing to my failure to establish any definite unit of time, and I found that that made very artificial any attempt to state the theory precisely. So, after writing out many chapters along what were evidently the Swedish lines, I scrapped the lot and felt that my new treatment was much safer and sounder from the logical point of view" (*JMK* XIV, p. 184). Keynes repeated this statement in his 1937 lectures, from which some of his own rough notes have survived (*JMK* XIV, p. 180). In these notes, Keynes also states that he had expounded the theory of effective demand in the *General Theory* on the assumption that "short-period expectations are always fulfilled"—by which I think he meant the assumption that the economy is always at the short-run equilibrium position determined by the intersection of the aggregate demand and supply curves. Keynes went on to say that were he to rewrite the book, he would add a chapter "showing what difference it makes when short-period expectations are disappointed"—and that though in the early stages of writing the *General Theory* he "regard[ed] this difference as important . . . [he] eventually . . . felt it to be of secondary importance, emphasis on it obscuring the real argument. For the theory of effective demand is substantially the same if we assume that short-period expectations are always fulfilled" (*JMK* XIV, p. 181; see also p. 183).

5. See Keynes' replies to Ohlin as presented in his 1937 *Economic Journal* articles, "Alternative Theories of the Rate of Interest" and "The 'Ex Ante' theory of the Rate of Interest." These are respectively reproduced on pp. 201–15 and 215–23 of *JMK* XIV.

6. As is well known, the futility of this debate had already been demonstrated in Hicks's 1936 review article. But that this had had no influence on Keynes is clear from his letter of February 1937 to Ohlin in which he denounced as "fundamental heresy" the idea that the rate of interest is "established by the demand and supply for credit" (*JMK* XIV, pp. 185–86). See also Hicks's *Value and Capital* (1939), p. 162, n. 1. The reader will recall the similar religious fervor with which Keynes had denounced Harrod's attempt (in their 1935 correspondence) to qualify Keynes' statement that the rate of interest was determined solely by the quantity of money (see Chapter 10 on p. 99, the quotation from Keynes' letter).

7. Entitled "The General Theory of Employment" and reproduced on pp. 109–23 of *JMK* XIV.

this symposium by Viner, Robertson, Leontief, and Taussig and concentrates instead on a "re-expression" of the two basic points with respect to which Keynes feels that his argument in the *General Theory* is "most clearly departing from previous theories" (*JMK* XIV, pp. 111–12). These points are, first, the fact that uncertainty pervades economic life and that this in turn is the cause of liquidity-preference, as well as of the fact that the "volume of investment . . . should fluctuate widely from time to time" (*JMK* XIV, p. 118); and second, the theory of effective demand, which is based on the investment and liquidity-preference functions so determined, supplemented by a propensity to consume that reflects the "psychological law . . . that when aggregate income increases, consumption expenditure will also increase but to a somewhat lesser extent" (*JMK* XIV, pp. 119–20).

Keynes' restatement of these two points in his *Quarterly Journal* article is indeed excellent; but it remains nevertheless a restatement, and not a modification, of the *General Theory*. In particular, there is little, if anything, in Keynes' discussion of the formation of expectations under uncertainty in this article that is not to be found in Chapter 12 of the *General Theory*, "The State of Long-Term Expectations." Thus Keynes' emphasis in the *Quarterly Journal* article that the uncertainty which characterizes so much of economic life is one for which "there is no scientific basis on which to form any calculable probability whatever" (*JMK* XIV, p. 114) does not in substance differ from his emphasis in Chapter 12 of the *General Theory* that, in view of the great uncertainty about the future, "our decisions to do something positive . . . can only be taken as a result of animal spirits . . . and not as the outcome of a weighted average of quantitative benefits multiplied by quantitative probabilities" (*GT* p. 161).[8]

In order to place things in their proper perspective, let me also remind the reader that the nonprobabilistic nature of economic uncertainty which Keynes emphasized in both these writings had been emphasized long before by Frank Knight in his classic *Risk, Uncertainty, and Profit* (1921). Let me also point out that Keynes does not really make much analytical use of this uncertainty. Thus, as already indicated, the only operational conclusions that he bases on it are the relatively general ones that (a) there is a speculative demand for money which depends inversely on the rate of interest (a conclusion which in large part Keynes had already reached in the *Treatise*) and

---

8. See also Keynes' statement in the *General Theory* that "by 'very uncertain' I do not mean the same thing as 'very improbable' "—a statement which he supports with a reference to Chap. 6 of his *Treatise on Probability* (*GT* p. 148, n. 1).

(b) there are wide fluctuations in the volume of investment, and this in turn is one of the major causes of the business cycle (a proposition which had been a commonplace for students of the cycle for many years). In neither the *General Theory* nor the 1937 article in the *Quarterly Journal of Economics*, however, does Keynes develop a theory of economic behavior under uncertainty.[9]

Having discussed until now only Keynes' reactions to the criticisms that were made of the *General Theory*, I think it important to emphasize that the material of *JMK* XIV shows us Keynes not only defending the existing ideas but also continuously open to new ideas and developments. Thus, for example, we find him in the fall of 1936 and spring of 1937 discussing with Joan Robinson and Roy Harrod their extensions of his theory to international trade and the trade cycle, respectively (*JMK* XIV, pp. 134–79). And what is most revealing about the nature of the ever-active mind of the man, we find him already in August 1936 writing to Hawtrey about tentative plans to produce a book of "Footnotes to 'The General Theory,' " "dealing with various criticisms and particular points which want carrying further," and even preparing a table of contents for it (*JMK* XIV, pp. 47, 133–34). From this table of contents it would appear that Keynes thought of this book as one that would provide a clearer and perhaps simpler exposition of the main ideas of the *General Theory*.[10] Again, in April 1937 he wrote Joan Robinson: "I am gradually getting myself into an outside position towards the book, and am feeling my way to new lines of exposition" (*JMK* XIV, p. 150). But the serious heart attack that he suffered shortly afterwards apparently put a halt to these plans (Harrod 1951, pp. 479–81; E. A. G. Robinson 1947, p. 63).

Keynes did recover sufficiently to carry out a vigorous debate with Tinbergen on the methodological problems of econometrics—a debate that ultimately led to a published exchange in the *Economic Journal* (*JMK* XIV, pp. 285–320).[11] And in the second half of 1938 he also carried out an intensive correspondence with Harrod on the

9. Which is probably one of the reasons why Paul Samuelson concluded many years ago that the *General Theory* "paves the way for a theory of expectation, but it hardly provides one" (1946, p. 320). See also the article by A. G. Hart, "Keynes' Analysis of Expectations and Uncertainty" (1947), to which Samuelson refers at this point.

10. This is also the view of Austin Robinson (E. A. G. Robinson, 1972, pp. 539–40). See also the interesting parallel which Moggridge draws with the draft table of contents that Keynes prepared in 1921 for his *Revision of the Treaty*, the "sequel" to his *Economic Consequences of the Peace* (*JMK* XIV, p. 133; *JMK* III, p. xiii). See also the actual preface to this "sequel" (*JMK* III, p. xv).

11. I discuss some aspects of this exchange in my forthcoming "Keynes and Econometrics" (1976).

growth model which the latter developed in his seminal "Essay in Dynamic Theory" (*JMK* XIV, pp. 320–50). But there are no further references in *JMK* XIV, which ends with material from December 1938, to the aforementioned book of "Footnotes."

And then came the war and the complete absorption of Keynes in the heavy governmental responsibilities that he undertook—both during the war and afterwards. And then his death in 1946.

The *Treatise*, as we have seen, began as a systematization of the *Tract*; and the *General Theory* as a "short book" to develop the theory of the *Treatise*. To the extent that it is meaningful to speculate about such matters, I do not, however, feel that a corresponding far-reaching metamorphosis would have taken place with respect to Keynes' planned "Footnotes to 'The General Theory.' "[12]

In part, this view reflects the fact that in his replies to his critics during 1936 and 1937, Keynes (as we have just seen) departed very little from the existing *General Theory*; and this stands in sharp contrast with his reactions during 1930 and 1931 to the criticisms of the *Treatise*. Again, in 1940 Keynes proceeded in his *How to Pay for the War*[13] to make use of the same theory of effective demand that he had developed in the *General Theory* in order to analyze the new problems of overemployment and inflation that were then being generated. Finally, in the years immediately following the publication of the *General Theory*, the initiative for significantly extending its analysis came (as we have seen), not from Keynes himself, but from the representatives of the younger generation, Joan Robinson and Roy Harrod. And this, I think, is the natural way that progress beyond the *General Theory* would have continued—as indeed it did.

12. In all honesty, I should point out that this conjecture differs from the one hinted at in my recent review article (1975, p. 268 bottom).
13. Reproduced on pp. 367–439 of *JMK* IX; see esp. pp. 372–77.

Bibliography

Angell, James W. "Monetary Theory and Monetary Policy: Some Recent Discussions." *Quarterly Journal of Economics* 39 (Feb. 1925): 267–99.

Ashley, W. "A Retrospect of Free-Trade Doctrine." *Economic Journal* 34 (Dec. 1924): 501–39.

Ashworth, William. *An Economic History of England 1870–1939*. London: Methuen, 1960.

Barro, R. J., and H. I. Grossman. "A General Disequilibrium Model of Income and Employment." *American Economic Review* 61 (March 1971): 82–93.

Bryce, R. B. Notes on Keynes' Lectures 1932/33, 1933/34, 1934/35. Typescript in the Keynes Papers (typed in recent years from the original handwritten notes in the possession of R. B. Bryce), in the Marshall Library of the University of Cambridge.

Champernowne, D. G. "Unemployment, Basic and Monetary: The Classical Analysis and the Keynesian." *Review of Economic Studies* 3 (June 1936): 201–16. As reprinted in Lekachman (1964), pp. 153–73.

Clower, Robert. "The Keynesian Counterrevolution: A Theoretical Appraisal." In *The Theory of Interest Rates*, edited by F. H. Hahn and F. P. R. Brechling (London: Macmillan, 1965), pp. 103–25.

Committee on Finance and Industry (Macmillan Committee). Unpublished minutes: 20 February 1930, 21 February 1930, 28 February 1930, 6 March 1930, 7 March 1930. In the Keynes Papers.

Davidson, Paul. "More on the Aggregate Supply Function." *Economic Journal* 72 (June 1962): 452–57.

———. *Money and the Real World*. London: Macmillan, 1972.

——— and Eugene Smolensky. *Aggregate Supply and Demand Analysis*. New York: Harper and Row, 1964.

Davis, J. Ronnie. *The New Economics and the Old Economists*. Ames, Iowa: The Iowa State University Press, 1971.

de Jong, F. J. "Supply Functions in Keynesian Economics." *Economic Journal* 64 (March 1954): 3–24.

———. "Keynes and Supply Functions: Second Rejoinder, with a Note on the Concept of Monetary Equilibrium." *Economic Journal* 65 (Sept. 1955): 479–84.

Dillard, Dudley. *The Economics of John Maynard Keynes: The Theory of a Monetary Economy*. New York: Prentice-Hall, 1948.

Eshag, Eprime. *From Marshall to Keynes: An Essay on the Monetary Theory of the Cambridge School*. Oxford: Blackwell, 1963.

F[ay], C. R. "[Obituary of] Frederick Lavington." *Economic Journal* 37 (Sept. 1927): 503–5.

Fisher, Irving. *The Rate of Interest*. New York: Macmillan, 1907.

———. *The Purchasing Power of Money*. New York: Macmillan, 1911.

———. *The Theory of Interest*. New York: Macmillan, 1930. Reprinted, New York: Kelley & Millman, 1954.

Galbraith, John Kenneth. "How Keynes Came to America." *New York Times Book Review*, 1965. As reprinted in *Essays on John Maynard*

Keynes, edited by Milo Keynes (Cambridge: Cambridge University Press, 1975), pp. 132–141.

Gregory, T. E. "Recent Theories of Currency Reform." *Economica* 4 (June 1924): 163–75.

Hansen, Alvin H. "A Fundamental Error in Keynes's 'Treatise on Money'." *American Economic Review* 22 (Sept. 1932): 462. As reprinted in *The Collected Writings of John Maynard Keynes*, Vol.V, pp. 329–30.

———. *A Guide to Keynes*. New York: McGraw-Hill, 1953.

Harrod, Roy F. "Mr. Keynes and Traditional Theory." *Econometrica* 5 (Jan. 1937): 74–86. As reprinted in Lekachman (1964), pp. 124–39.

———. "An Essay in Dynamic Theory." *Economic Journal* 49 (March 1939): 14–33.

———. *The Life of John Maynard Keynes*. London: Macmillan, 1951. Reprinted, New York: Kelley, 1969.

Hart, Albert G. "Keynes' Analysis of Expectations and Uncertainty." In *The New Economics: Keynes' Influence on Theory and Public Policy*, edited by Seymour E. Harris (New York: Alfred A. Knopf, 1947).

Hawtrey, R. G. *Monetary Reconstruction*. London: Longmans, Green, 1922.

———. Review of *A Tract on Monetary Reform* by J. M. Keynes. *Economic Journal* 34 (June 1924): 227–35.

———. *The Art of Central Banking*. London: Longmans, Green, 1932.

———. *Capital and Employment*. London: Longmans, Green, 1937.

———. "Keynes and Supply Functions." *Economic Journal* 64 (Dec. 1954): 834–39; 66 (Sept. 1956): 482–84.

Hayek, F. A. von. "Reflections on the Pure Theory of Money of Mr. J. M. Keynes." *Economica* 11 (Aug. 1931): 270–95; 12 (Feb. 1932): 22–44.

Hicks, John R. "A Suggestion for Simplifying the Theory of Money." *Economica* 2 (Feb. 1935): 1–19.

———. "Mr. Keynes' Theory of Employment." *Economic Journal* 46 (June 1936): 238–53.

———. "Mr. Keynes and the 'Classics'; a Suggested Interpretation." *Econometrica* 5 (April 1937): 147–59. As reprinted in *Readings in the Theory of Income Distribution*, by The American Economic Association (Philadelphia: Blakiston, 1946), pp. 461–476.

———. *Value and Capital*. Oxford: Clarendon Press, 1939.

———. "Dennis Holme Robertson, 1890–1963: A Memoir." In Sir Dennis Robertson, *Essays in Money and Interest*, selected by Sir John Hicks (Manchester: Collins, 1966), pp. 9–22.

———. *Critical Essays in Monetary Theory*. Oxford: Oxford University Press, 1967.

———. "Recollections and Documents." *Economica* 40 (Feb. 1973): 2–11.

Howson, Susan, and Donald Winch. *The Economic Advisory Council 1930–1939*. Cambridge: Cambridge University Press (forthcoming, 1976).

Hutchison, T. W. *A Review of Economic Doctrines 1870–1929*. Oxford: Clarendon Press, 1953.

———. *Economics and Economic Policy in Britain 1946–1966: Some Aspects of Their Inter-relations*. London: George Allen and Unwin, 1968.

Johannsen, N. *A Neglected Point in Connection with Crises*. New York: The Bankers Publishing Co., 1908. Reprinted, New York: Kelley, 1971.

Kahn, Alfred E. *Great Britain in the World Economy*. New York: Columbia University Press, 1946.

Kahn, Richard F. "The Relation of Home Investment to Unemployment." *Economic Journal* 41 (June 1931): 173–98. As reprinted in Kahn (1972), pp. 1–27.

————. *Selected Essays on Employment and Growth*. Cambridge: Cambridge University Press, 1972.

Keynes, John M.[1] Review of *The Purchasing Power of Money: Its Determination and Relation to Credit, Interest, and Crisis*, by Irving Fisher. *Economic Journal* 21 (Sept. 1911): 393–99.

————. *Indian Currency and Finance*. 1913. As reprinted in Keynes' *Collected Writings*, Vol. I.

————. *The Economic Consequences of the Peace*. 1919. As reprinted in Keynes' *Collected Writings*, Vol. II.

————. *A Treatise on Probability*. 1921. As reprinted in Keynes' *Collected Writings*, Vol. VIII.

————. *A Revision of the Treaty*. 1922. As reprinted in Keynes' *Collected Writings*, Vol. III.

————. *A Tract on Monetary Reform*. 1923. As reprinted in Keynes' *Collected Writings*, Vol. IV.

————. *Monetary Reform*. New York: Harcourt, Brace, 1924. (U.S. edition of the preceding, with different pagination.)

————. *The Economic Consequences of Mr. Churchill* (1925). As reprinted in Keynes' *Collected Writings*, Vol. IX, pp. 207–30.

————. "The German Transfer Problem." *Economic Journal* 39 (March 1929): 1–7. As reprinted in *Readings in the Theory of International Trade*, by The American Economic Association (Philadelphia: Blakiston, 1949), pp. 161–69.

————. *A Treatise on Money, Vol. I: The Pure Theory of Money*. 1930. As reprinted in Keynes' *Collected Writings*, Vol. V.

————. *A Treatise on Money, Vol. II: The Applied Theory of Money*. 1930. As reprinted in Keynes' *Collected Writings*, Vol. VI.

————. *Essays in Persuasion*. London: Macmillan, 1931.

————. *Essays in Persuasion*. 1931. As reprinted with additions in Keynes' *Collected Writings*, Vol. IX.

————. "Keynes's Fundamental Equations: A Note." *American Economic Review* 22 (Dec. 1932): 691. As reprinted in Keynes' *Collected Writings*, Vol. V, pp. 330–31.

————. *Essays in Biography*. 1933. As reprinted with additions in Keynes' *Collected Writings*, Vol. X.

————. *The Means to Prosperity*. 1933. As reprinted in Keynes' *Collected Writings*, Vol. IX, pp. 335–66.

————. *The General Theory of Employment, Interest, and Money*. 1936. As reprinted in Keynes' *Collected Writings*, Vol. VII.

————. *How to Pay for the War*. 1940. As reprinted in Keynes' *Collected Writings*, Vol. IX, pp. 367–439.

————. *The General Theory and After, Part I: Preparation*. Edited by Donald Moggridge. Vol. XIII of Keynes' *Collected Writings*, 1973.

————. *The General Theory and After, Part II: Defence and Development*.

---

1. Published articles of Keynes which are reproduced in *JMK* XIII and XIV have not been listed here.

Edited by Donald Moggridge. Vol. XIV of Keynes' *Collected Writings*, 1973.

————. *Collected Writings*. London: Macmillan, for the Royal Economic Society, 1971–1973.

———— and Hubert Henderson. *Can Lloyd George Do It?: An Examination of the Liberal Pledge*. 1929. As reprinted in Keynes' *Collected Writings*, Vol. IX, pp. 86–125.

Klein, Lawrence R. *The Keynesian Revolution*. New York: Macmillan, 1947.

Knight, Frank H. *Risk, Uncertainty, and Profit*. New York: Houghton Mifflin, 1921.

————. "Interest." *The Encyclopedia of the Social Sciences*. New York: Macmillan, 1932. As reprinted in *The Ethics of Competition and Other Essays* (New York: Harper and Brothers, 1935).

————. "The Quantity of Capital and the Rate of Interest." *Journal of Political Economy* 44 (Aug. and Oct. 1936): 433–63, 612–42.

Lambert, Paul. "The Evolution of Keynes's Thought from the Treatise on Money to the General Theory." *Annals of Public and Co-operative Economy* 40 (July–Sept. 1969): 243–63.

Lavington, Frederick. *The English Capital Market*. London: Methuen, 1921. Reprinted, New York: Kelley, 1968.

————. *The Trade Cycle: An Account of the Causes Producing Rhythmical Changes in the Activity of Business*. London: P. S. King and Staples, 1922.

Leijonhufvud, Axel. *On Keynesian Economics and the Economics of Keynes*. New York: Oxford University Press, 1968.

Lekachman, Robert, editor. *Keynes' General Theory: Reports of Three Decades*. New York: St. Martin's Press, 1964.

Leontief, Wassily W. "The Fundamental Assumption of Mr. Keynes' Monetary Theory of Unemployment." *Quarterly Journal of Economics* 51 (Nov. 1936): 192–97.

Lerner, Abba P. "The General Theory." *International Labour Review* 34 (1936): 435–54. As reprinted in Lekachman (1964), pp. 203–22.

Macmillan Committee. *See* Committee on Finance and Industry.

Marshall, Alfred. *Principles of Economics*. 8th edition. London: Macmillan, 1920.

————. *Money Credit and Commerce*. London: Macmillan, 1923.

————. *Official Papers*. London: Macmillan, 1926.

Mathias, Peter. *The First Industrial Nation: An Economic History of Britain 1700–1914*. London: Methuen, 1969.

Mill, John Stuart. *Principles of Political Economy*. 1st edition, 1848. New edition, edited by Sir W. A. Ashley. London: Longmans, Green, 1909.

Millar, James R. "The Social Accounting Basis of Keynes' Aggregate Supply and Demand Functions." *Economic Journal* 82 (June 1972): 600–11.

Mitchell, B. R., and P. Deane. *Abstract of British Historical Statistics*. Cambridge: Cambridge University Press, 1962.

Modigliani, Franco. "Liquidity Preference and the Theory of Interest and Money." *Econometrica* 12 (Jan. 1944): 45–88.

Moggridge, D. E. *British Monetary Policy 1924–1931: The Norman Conquest of $4.86*. Cambridge: Cambridge University Press, 1972.

————. "From the *Treatise* to *The General Theory*: An Exercise in Chronology." *History of Political Economy* 5 (Spring 1973): 72–88.

―――― and Susan Howson. "Keynes on Monetary Policy, 1910–1946." *Oxford Economic Papers* 26 (July 1974): 226–47.

Myrdal, Gunnar. *Monetary Equilibrium*. London: W. Hodge, 1939. Translated from the German edition of 1933, which is a revision and enlargement of the original Swedish version of 1931.

[Nurkse, Ragnar]. *International Currency Experience: Lessons of the Inter-War Period*. League of Nations, 1944.

Ohlin, Bertil. "The Reparation Problem: A Discussion." *Economic Journal* 39 (June 1929): 172–73. As reprinted in *Readings on the Theory of International Trade*, by The American Economic Association (Philadelphia: Blakiston, 1969), pp. 170–78.

――――. "Some Notes on the Stockholm Theory of Saving and Investment." *Economic Journal* 47 (March and June 1937): 53–69, 221–40. As reprinted in *Readings in Business Cycle Theory*, by The American Economic Association (Philadelphia: Blakiston, 1944), pp. 87–130.

Owens, Richard N. Review of *A Tract on Monetary Reform* by J. M. Keynes. *Journal of Political Economy* 52 (1924): 730–31.

Patinkin, Don. "Price Flexibility and Full Employment." *American Economic Review* 38 (Sept. 1948): 543–64. Reprinted with revisions in *Readings in Monetary Theory*, edited by F. A. Lutz and L. W. Mints (Philadelphia: Blakiston, 1951).

――――. "Involuntary Unemployment and the Keynesian Supply Function." *Economic Journal* 59 (Sept. 1949): 360–83.

――――. *Money, Interest, and Prices*. Evanston, Ill.. Row, Peterson, 1956. 2d edition, New York: Harper and Row, 1965.

――――. "Demand Curves and Consumer's Surplus." In *Measurement in Economics: Studies in Mathematical Economics and Econometrics in Memory of Yehuda Grunfeld*, by Carl Christ and others (Stanford: Stanford University Press, 1963), pp. 83–112.

――――. "Money and Wealth: A Review Article." *Journal of Economic Literature* 7 (Dec. 1969): 1140–60.

――――. "The Chicago Tradition, the Quantity Theory, and Friedman." *Journal of Money, Credit and Banking* 1 (Feb. 1969): 46–70. As reprinted in *Studies in Monetary Economics*, by Don Patinkin (New York: Harper and Row, 1972), pp. 92–117.

――――. "Keynesian Monetary Theory and the Cambridge School." In *Issues in Monetary Economics*, edited by H. G. Johnson and A. R. Nobay (Oxford: Oxford University Press, 1974), pp. 3–30.

――――. "The Role of the 'Liquidity Trap' in Keynesian Economics." *Banca Nazionale del Lavoro Quarterly Review*, no.108 (March 1974): 3–11.

――――. "The Collected Writings of John Maynard Keynes: From the *Tract* to the *General Theory*." *Economic Journal* 85 (June 1975): 249–70.

――――. "Keynes and Econometrics: On the Interaction Between Macroeconomic Theory and Measurement in the Interwar Period." *Econometrica* 44 (1976). Forthcoming.

Pesek, Boris P., and Thomas R. Saving. *Money, Wealth and Economic Theory*. New York: Macmillan, 1967.

Pigou, A. C. "The Value of Money." *Quarterly Journal of Economics* 32 (1917–18): 38–65. As reprinted in *Readings in Monetary Theory*, edited by F. A. Lutz and L. W. Mints (Philadelphia: Blakiston, 1951), pp. 162–83.

――――. *The Theory of Unemployment*. London: Macmillan, 1933.

————. "Mr. J. M. Keynes' General Theory of Employment, Interest and Money." *Economica,* 3 (May 1936): 115–32.

————. *Keynes's 'General Theory': A Retrospective View.* London: Macmillan, 1950.

Reddaway, W. B. "The General Theory of Employment, Interest, and Money." *Economic Record* 12 (June 1936). As reprinted in Lekachman (1964), pp. 99–107.

Robbins, Lionel. *Autobiography of an Economist.* London: Macmillan, 1971.

Robertson, D. H. *A Study of Industrial Fluctuation: An Enquiry into the Character and Causes of the So-Called Movements of Trade.* London: P. S. King and Son, 1915.

————. *Money.* 1st edition, 1922. Revised ed., London: Nisbet and Co., 1928.

————. *Banking Policy and the Price Level.* London: P. S. King and Co., 1926. Reprinted with a new introduction, New York: Kelley, 1949.

————. "Industrial Fluctuation and the Natural Rate of Interest." *Economic Journal* 44 (Dec. 1934): 650–56.

————. "Some Notes on Mr. Keynes' General Theory of Employment." *Quarterly Journal of Economics* 51 (Nov. 1936): 168–91.

————. "Alternative Theories of the Rate of Interest." *Economic Journal* 47 (Sept. 1937): 428–36.

————. *Essays in Monetary Theory.* London: Staples Press, 1940.

———— and H. G. Johnson. "Keynes and Supply Functions." *Economic Journal* 65 (Sept. 1955): 474–78.

Robinson, E. A. G. "John Maynard Keynes 1883–1946." *Economic Journal* 57 (March 1947): 1–68. As reprinted in Lekachman (1964), pp. 13–86.

————. "John Maynard Keynes: Economist, Author, Statesman." *Economic Journal* 82 (June 1972): 531–46.

Robinson, Joan. "A Parable on Savings and Investment." *Economica* 13 (Feb. 1933): 75–84.

————. "The Theory of Money and the Analysis of Output." *Review of Economic Studies* 1 (Oct. 1933): 22–26. As reprinted in *Collected Economic Papers* by Joan Robinson (Oxford: Blackwell, 1951), 1: 52–58.

————. *The Economics of Imperfect Competition.* London: Macmillan, 1933.

————. *Introduction to the Theory of Employment.* London: Macmillan, 1937.

————. *Collected Economic Papers,* Vol. 1. Oxford: Blackwell, 1951.

————. "Introduction" to *Studies in the Theory of Business Cycles 1933–1939,* by Michal Kalecki (Oxford: Blackwell, 1966).

————. "What Has Become of the Keynesian Revolution?" In *After Keynes,* edited by Joan Robinson (Oxford: Blackwell, 1973), pp. 1–11.

Samuelson, Paul A. "Lord Keynes and the General Theory." *Econometrica* 14 (1946): 187–200. As reprinted in Lekachman (1964), pp. 315–31.

————. "Irving Fisher and the Theory of Capital". In *Ten Economic Studies in the Tradition of Irving Fisher,* W. Fellner et al. (New York: John Wiley and Sons, 1967).

Schumpeter, Joseph A. *The Theory of Economic Development.* Cambridge, Mass.: Harvard University Press, 1934.

————. *A History of Economic Analysis.* New York: Oxford University Press, 1954.

Shackle, G. L. S. *The Years of High Theory: Invention and Tradition in*

Economic Thought 1926–1939. Cambridge: Cambridge University Press, 1967.

Sprague, O. M. W. Review of *Monetary Reform* by J. M. Keynes. *American Economic Review* 14 (Dec. 1924): 770–71.

Stein, Herbert. *The Fiscal Revolution in America*. Chicago: University of Chicago Press, 1969.

Taussig, F. W. "Employment and the National Dividend." *Quarterly Journal of Economics* 51 (Nov. 1936): 198–203.

U.S. Bureau of the Census. *Historical Statistics of the United States, Colonial Times to 1957*. Washington, D.C., 1960.

Viner, Jacob. "Mr. Keynes on the Causes of Unemployment." *Quarterly Journal of Economics* 51 (Nov. 1936): 147–67. As reprinted in Lekachman (1964), pp. 235–53.

Walras, Léon. *Elements of Pure Economics*. Translated from the definitive edition (1926) by William Jaffé. London: Allen and Unwin, 1954. For the present purposes, the 1926 definitive edition is equivalent to the 4th edition of 1900.

Weintraub, Sidney. "The Micro-Foundations of Aggregate Demand and Supply." *Economic Journal* 67 (Sept. 1957): 455–70.

———. *An Approach to the Theory of Income Distribution*. Philadelphia: Chilton, 1958.

———. *Classical Keynesianism, Monetary Theory and the Price Level*. Philadelphia: Chilton, 1961.

Wells, P. J. "Aggregate Supply and Demand: An Explanation of Chapter III of *The General Theory*." *Canadian Journal of Economics and Political Science*, 28 (Nov. 1962): 585–90.

Wicksell, Knut. *Interest and Prices* (1898). Translated by R. F. Kahn. London: Macmillan, 1936.

———. *Lectures on Political Economy: Vol. II. Money* (1906). Translated by E. Classen. London: George Routledge and Sons, 1935.

Winch, Donald. *Economics and Policy: A Historical Study*. London: Hodder and Stoughton, 1969.

Wright, Harold. *Population*. Cambridge Economic Handbooks, V. Cambridge: Cambridge University Press, 1923.

W[right], H[arold]. "[Obituary of] Frederick Lavington." *Economic Journal* 37 (Sept. 1927): 503–5.

Youngson, A. J. *Britain's Economic Growth 1920–1966*. New York: Kelley, 1967.

Index of references to
Keynes' published writings

Publications have been listed in chronological order. Full bibliographical information is provided only for publications not listed in the Bibliography; see p. 146 n. above. For the *Tract*, the *Treatise*, and the *General Theory*, this index includes only the references to specific pages.

Pages where cited
in this book

Review of Irving Fisher's *Purchasing Power of Money*
(1911)   12, 46

Indian Currency and Finance (1913)   19n, 24n

Economic Consequences of the Peace (1919)   15

Treatise on Probability (1921)   24n, 141n

Revision of the Treaty (1922)   15

Tract on Monetary Reform (1923)

New ed. (1971) pages	Original ed. (1923) pages	U.S. ed. (1924) pages	
3	3	5	16
4–7	5–8	7–11	19, 36n
11–12	12–13	14–16	36n
16–17	17	20–21	19, 36n
30	32	36	123
43–45	48–51	54–57	11n
45–46	51–53	57–59	14
50–52	58–62	64–68	15
61–70	74–87	81–95	11, 26
63	77	84–85	26
63 n1	78 n1	85 n1	11
64	78	86	27
65	80	88	25
81–86	97–104	106–12	14
83	103	113	21
87	105	115	21
119	145	158	123
120	146–47	158–59	15
138	172–73	187	124
140	176	190	124
141–46	177–85	192–201	123
147–49	186–89	202–5	125
152	193–94	209–10	123, 124
153	196	212	124

		Pages where cited in this book
Tract on Monetary Reform (French ed., 1924)		15
Economic Consequences of Mr. Churchill (1925)		16n

Can Lloyd George Do It? (1929)   18

New ed. (1972) pages	Original ed. (1929) pages	
104–7	23–26	71, 129, 131–32
118–19	36–38	128n

| "The German Transfer Problem" (1929) | | 129 |

Treatise on Money (1930), Vol. I

New ed. (1971) pages	Original ed. (1930) pages	
xvii	vi	54
xviii	vi–vii	29, 30, 54
30–32	34–36	41
55	62	16n
120	133	13, 36, 46
122–23	135–36	35, 38
125	138–39	36, 51, 55
126	139–40	33
127–31	140–46	37n, 38–39, 40–41, 50, 51
131–33	146–48	31, 46
134–35	149–50	46n
137–38	152–54	46
139	154–55	36–37, 47
141	157	123
144	160–61	51–52
145	161	51
147	164	129
148	164–65	129, 133
151	168–69	13, 37, 94, 123
159–60	177–78	67
163	181–82	33, 45n
167–76	186–96	36, 124
171–73	191–94	36, 47
176 n3	197 n3	48
177 n3	198 n3	47
178 n2	199 n2	49n
191–93	213–16	129
200	223–24	42
207–8	231–32	41
211–12	236–37	46n
218	244	46n
222	248–49	37n
223–24	250	39–40
229–30	256–57	40
239–41	266–69	40, 44, 45, 53
241–46	269–75	122

154

Pagination of the original and the new (1973) editions of *The General Theory* is practically identical, except for Preface.

Index of names

For convenience, publications are frequently referred to by abbreviated titles.

158

Index of subjects